DEPARTMENT OF EDUCATION AND SCIENCE

The Education of Deaf Children:

The Possible Place of Finger Spelling and Signing

*Report of the Committee
appointed by the Secretary of
State for Education and
Science in October,* 1964

LONDON
HER MAJESTY'S STATIONERY OFFICE
1968

First Published 1968
Third impression 1973

The estimated cost of the preparation of this Report is £3,883 6s. 3d. of which £882 13s. 0d. represents the estimated cost of printing and publishing the report.

SBN 11 270003 9

Foreword

I welcome this most useful report, which represents the first attempt in this country to look dispassionately at a subject which has proved highly contentious in the past among deaf people and those who work with them.

There is an immense amount of good will and dedicated effort given to work in all fields with deaf people. The keenness of the discussion among teachers, university staffs, medical officers, social workers and the deaf themselves about the media of communication in education was an indication of their deep concern to offer deaf children the best possible education for their social and personal development. For this reason, I believe that all will value greatly the careful analysis of the problem and the guidance which the Committee has provided indicating areas where further research is necessary.

Edward Short

12th February, 1968

Dear Secretary of State,

In October 1964, your predecessor appointed us with the request to consider the place, if any, of finger spelling and signing in the education of deaf children.

I have pleasure in submitting the Report of the Committee. We began our work knowing that the education of deaf children had long been a field of controversy; and we are happy to be able to record that we found a notable approach to unanimity on fundamental questions among our witnesses and ourselves. We believe that the main unifying influence has been a common concern for the children.

It is our hope that our review of informed opinion and our recommendations will help to clarify some of the problems of the education of the children and to promote measures conducive to their welfare.

I am, Yours sincerely,

M. M. LEWIS
(Chairman)

The Right Hon. Patrick Gordon Walker, P.C., M.P.

Membership of the Committee

Professor M. M. Lewis (Chairman), Emeritus Professor of Education, University of Nottingham, formerly Director of the University Institute of Education.

Mrs. R. M. Clare, Royal School for Deaf Children, Margate.

Dr. J. C. Denmark, Consultant Psychiatrist, Manchester Regional Hospital Board.

Mr. P. Gaskill, Principal, Royal Cross School for the Deaf, Preston.

Mrs. S. M. Gray, University of London Institute of Education.

Mr. R. Gulliford, Education Department, University of Birmingham.

The Right Reverend Monsignor Canon J. J. Kelly, V.G., Principal, St. John's Residential School for the Deaf, Boston Spa.

Dr. T. S. Littler, formerly of the Medical Research Council Wernher Research Unit on Deafness, King's College Hospital Medical School.

Dr. K. P. Murphy, Deputy Director, Audiology Unit, Royal Berkshire Hospital, Reading.

Miss N. L. North, Head Mistress, Braidwood School, Birmingham.

Mr. M. M. Reed, Inspector of Special Education, Inner London Education Authority.

Mr. G. E. Robinson, Principal, the College of Deaf Welfare.

Mrs. E. M. Sheavyn, formerly Youth Organiser and Education Officer, British Deaf and Dumb Association.

Mr. H. H. Shorrock, Head Master, Longwill School, Birmingham.

Professor I. G. Taylor, Ellis Llwyd Jones Professor of Audiology and Education of the Deaf, University of Manchester.

Professor M. D. Vernon, until September, 1967, Professor of Psychology University of Reading.

Mr. G. W. W. Browne, Department of Education and Science, Assessor (until March, 1966).

Mr. D. E. Lloyd Jones, Department of Education and Science, Assessor (from April, 1966).

Dr. E. E. Simpson, Senior Medical Officer, Department of Education and Science, Assessor.

Mr. W. H. Snowdon, H.M.I., Assessor.

Mr. D. S. Petrie, H.M.I. Observer on behalf of the Scottish Education Department.

Miss J. M. Scrimshaw, Department of Education and Science, Secretary.

Mr. M. B. Baker, Department of Education and Science, Assistant Secretary (until February, 1965).

Miss B. P. Lincoln, Department of Education and Science, Assistant Secretar (from March, 1965).

Contents

Note of reservation

Note by the Chairman

Appendices

Tables and Graph

Terms of Reference

'To consider the place, if any, of finger spelling and
signing in the education of the deaf.'

Introduction

1. We were appointed in October 1964, by the Secretary of State for Education and Science, with the following terms of reference:

'To consider the place, if any, of finger spelling and signing in the education of the deaf'.

2. We came to this task as individuals interested in the subject. Some of us are concerned professionally with the deaf, but none of us, as a member of the Committee, represents the viewpoint of an organisation or association working with or for deaf children or adults. Our collective experience includes the education of deaf and partially hearing children, the fields of psychology and psychiatry, both generally and with special reference to the problems of deafness, the welfare of deaf adolescents and adults, and university research and teacher training concerned with handicapped children in general and deaf and partially hearing children in particular. One of us is a person deaf from birth who received valuable help throughout our deliberations from interpreters using finger spelling and signing to supplement reception through lipreading.

3. We have met in full Committee on 36 days and a Sub-Committee has held a further 12 meetings. A list of organisations and individuals who gave oral evidence or submitted memoranda to us is in Appendix A. In addition we received many letters from members of the public whose interest in deaf children had been stimulated either by their own or their children's deafness or by professional or social contact with deaf people.

4. Miss C. Brooke-Hughes, a Welfare Officer of the Ministry of Health, assisted us by interviewing young deaf people who had left school in the years 1956 to 1965. For this purpose she used a questionnaire devised by the Committee.

5. Lady Paget, assisted by three teachers of the deaf, arranged at our request demonstrations of the systematic sign language devised by the late Sir Richard Paget and further developed by Lady Paget and Dr. Pierre Gorman. The Reverend Canon T. H. Sutcliffe and Mr. K. Scarratt demonstrated the use of finger spelling, with some examples of signs.

6. Mr. H. G. Williams, a member of H.M. Inspectorate and formerly a teacher of the deaf, carried out for us a survey of relevant foreign literature and research work with special reference to that of the U.S.A. and the U.S.S.R. In addition, material was sent to us from abroad, including memoranda from the Clarke School for the Deaf, Massachusetts, and Gallaudet College, Washington D.C., the American university for the deaf.

7. We had the privilege of being addressed by Dr. Powrie Vaux Doctor, Editor of American Annals of the Deaf, on the methods of communication used at Gallaudet College, by Professor Stephen Quigley, Professor of Special Education in the Institute of Research on Exceptional Children at the University of Illinois, on the progress of the research under his direction into the use of finger spelling in teaching young deaf children, and by Professor Hans Furth of the Catholic University of America on his work on language and the development of thinking.

8. We are grateful to all those who have helped us, but perhaps we may express a particular debt of gratitude to those deaf people, both young and old, who have

written to tell us their opinions. It was not easy for some of our deaf correspondents to put their thoughts in writing and the fact that they took the trouble to do so testifies to the strength of their concern.

9. The rest of the Committee wish to pay special tribute to the excellent help they have received from the Secretary, Miss J. M. Scrimshaw, at every stage and in every aspect of their work. Her drafting of papers from the diversity of material presented to us has been invaluable. In all this she has been ably assisted by Mr. M. B. Baker, until February, 1965, and from then onwards by Miss B. P. Lincoln. We offer them all our warm thanks.

Chapter I. The Scope and Procedure of the Enquiry

The subjects of the enquiry

1. The children whose education is the subject of our study are those classified as deaf pupils within the meaning of the definition in the Handicapped Pupils and Special Schools Amending Regulations, 1962[1] These regulations, like those[2] which they amend, define two categories of pupils with impaired hearing. The definitions read as follows:

'deaf pupils, that is to say, pupils with impaired hearing who require education by methods suitable for pupils with little or no naturally acquired speech or language;

partially hearing pupils, that is to say, pupils with impaired hearing whose development of speech and language, even if retarded, is following a normal pattern, and who require for their education special arrangements or facilities though not necessarily all the educational methods used for deaf pupils'.

2. These definitions do not distinguish between the categories by degree of hearing loss. Although this is an important factor governing decisions whether a child should be educated as a deaf or a partially hearing pupil, it is not the sole criterion. The distinction between the definitions is one relating to the development of speech and language since it is this which goes far to determine the educational methods which are appropriate for a child. Many factors in addition to hearing loss may affect the development of speech and language in a child with impaired hearing and we discuss these fully in Chapter V. It is sufficient to note here that it cannot be assumed that because a child has a severe hearing loss he will inevitably need to be educated as a deaf pupil or that because his hearing loss is less severe he will respond to special educational treatment as a partially hearing pupil. It has also to be borne in mind that educational arrangements for partially hearing pupils are closely related to and sometimes overlap with those made for deaf pupils and that the relationship is more complex than one arising simply from an organisational pattern. It also affects individual children in the sense that a child may properly be regarded as a deaf pupil at one stage of his school life and as a partially hearing pupil at another. For these reasons we have felt bound to consider the education of deaf pupils in the context of the educational arrangements made for all children with impaired hearing.

Influences in early childhood

3. The problems of educating pupils with impaired hearing cannot be fully understood if they are considered in isolation, without reference to what happens to children before and after school life. Any child entering school has already been influenced in many ways which may be either helpful or unhelpful to his personal development and educational progress. For a child who is born with an impairment of hearing, or who suffers such an impairment in infancy, the early years of life are probably the most critical since they may unalterably determine the pattern of his whole future life. A child whose hearing is normal and who has no other handicap affecting his ability to communicate learns to talk during these years by listening to others around him speaking and by hearing the sound of his own voice. Not only does he build up vocabulary, but

3

he assimilates effortlessly a remarkable command of the structure of language. If a child with impaired hearing is to acquire the power to speak and use language, special measures must be taken during the early years to help him. In our study we have therefore taken careful note of what happens to children with impaired hearing before they enter school and the effect this seems to have on their subsequent progress.

The effects of education on adult life

4. We have also looked beyond school in an attempt to evaluate educational methods by their effect on the lives of deaf pupils after they have left school. This seemed an obviously necessary and perhaps straightforward procedure likely to produce particularly meaningful results. In practice, however, there are difficulties in making an objective evaluation which is clearly relevant in terms of the developing work of the schools. The reason is that there is an increasing number of younger pupils with impaired hearing who, unlike their senior fellow pupils and preceding generations of school leavers, have received pre-school training after early diagnosis of hearing loss and whose parents were given skilled guidance in their management. An evaluation of the educational attainments of senior pupils or older deaf people is open to the comment that, irrespective of its intrinsic value, it is irrelevant as a guide to the attainments of future generations of school leavers, whose special educational treatment will have been different and more extensive. For this reason it can be argued that it would be wrong to base recommendations for the future upon such an evaluation; and we are bound to accept that there is some force in this argument.

5. It might be suggested that a more significant exercise would be to compare the attainments of school leavers today with those of deaf people who left school thirty or forty years ago for whom, similarly, there were no opportunities of early auditory training or other features of current practice, and who were, in some cases, educated in schools using manual media of communication. But such a comparison presents even more formidable difficulties because of the many variable factors involved. The difficulty of drawing any conclusions from reports of adults lies in the impossibility of contacting a representative sample of adult deaf people. Another factor is the change which has taken place in the student body of special schools for the deaf. Not only is there now a very substantial measure of separate provision for deaf and partially hearing pupils*, resulting in a concentration of the most severely handicapped pupils in the schools for the deaf, but there is also evidence of increased complexity of handicap among children classified as deaf pupils. In a paper read to a conference held in Oxford in 1963 on research into deafness, Mr. Gavin Livingstone, consultant E.N.T. surgeon, United Oxford Hospitals, pointed out, 'More children are surviving now because of better post-natal and ante-natal care and because of general improvements in the care of the handicapped. For this reason the number of children with dual handicap (e.g. deafness and cerebral palsy, deafness and low mental ability, deafness and various congenital malformations) is increasing'. At the same conference, describing a recent study of causes of deafness amongst 2,355 special school children Dr. G. S. Fraser, Department of Ophthalmological Research, Royal College of Surgeons, referred to changes which had occurred in causes and to further changes which

---

* See paragraph 14.

4

might be expected. 'In at least half the children the cause of deafness is the sequel of illness or prematurity or their treatment. In the past many such children would have died. In the future, as medical treatment improves it may be expected that they will recover completely without untoward sequelae such as deafness. The virtual eradication of otitis media as a cause of profound deafness in children is a case in point'[3]. A study of the changing causes of deafness can be made by reference to the works of such writers as Macleod Yearsley, Phyllis Kerridge, Edith Whetnall and D. B. Fry[4].

6. Faced with the dilemmas described above, we have felt bound to be cautious in drawing conclusions from an evaluation of present results as seen in the lives of the school leavers of today. Yet this is not a yardstick we would wish to discard since we do not believe that it is realistic to suppose that recent developments in special educational treatment, though they may substantially reduce the numbers of children with whom we are mainly concerned, will provide an answer to all problems. Indeed, the fact that schools for the deaf now contain a higher proportion of children with complex disabilities suggests that new ways must be sought to overcome their difficulties. Whether these should include the use of manual media of communication is the question to which we address ourselves.

Educational and clinical classification

7. Earlier in this chapter we were concerned to indicate the broad basis of educational classification. The purpose of such classification is to assemble children with impaired hearing in groups which are more or less homogeneous educationally even though in medical terms there may be significant differences between the individuals making up a group. Inevitably, in the education of handicapped children, questions arise about the point at which clinical heterogeneity calls for educational re-grouping and this is as true of schools for the deaf as of other special schools. We have already indicated that the disability from which some deaf pupils suffer is of a complex nature. It is also the case that schools for the deaf admit children with additional disabilities for whom it is not always possible to say at the outset which will prove to be the major educational handicap. For this reason the schools usually have on their roll, even if only temporarily, a number of children, administratively classified as deaf pupils, who may present more complex teaching problems than children whose major handicap is clearly one of hearing. Then again, it has to be borne in mind that hearing impairment itself is not of one kind alone. The defect may be in the peripheral mechanism of hearing, or in the nervous system, including the brain. These differences may have implications for the special educational treatment of individual pupils. Throughout our study it has been very evident that there is no such convenient entity as 'the deaf child'.

The procedure of the enquiry

8. Since our specific concern has been to consider whether finger spelling and signing should be included among the media of communication used in school with children classified as deaf, one of our first tasks was to attempt to discover the extent to which these media are used at present in teaching. This information was obtained partly from evidence given to us by individual teachers, but more comprehensively by questionnaire addressed to all the schools concerned. The results are reported in Chapter VI.

5

9. We then tried to accomplish the major part of our study by carrying out reviews of both informed opinion and objective evidence of the value of manual media of communication in education. For this purpose an open invitation to all who might wish to submit evidence was published in the press and appropriate journals, we ourselves invited individuals and organisations concerned with deaf children and adults professionally, deaf people and the parents of deaf children to send us their views and in some cases to appear before us in person. We also arranged for a review of relevant literature and through a Sub-Committee composed of members with experience in research we examined a number of research papers which might bear directly or indirectly on the subject of our study. We did not ourselves commission research because our enquiries failed to find a school in which finger spelling or signing was systematically used and which could have been adequately matched for control purposes with a similar school using oral methods. Summaries of opinion are contained in Chapters IX to XII. The results of our review of literature and research are in Chapter VII.

10. The last stage of our study involved an assessment of the evidence and opinions submitted in the light of an evaluation of the results now being achieved in the education of deaf pupils. We have already indicated that such an evaluation may be of limited use in so far as it concentrates on standards now being attained by school leavers. In addition we were conscious that an attempt to evaluate results presents many difficulties and we relied not only on our personal knowledge but also, so far as possible, on external sources. Our recommendations are based upon this assessment and upon what we hope is a realistic estimate of future developments in the special educational treatment of deaf pupils. The main body of our views and recommendations is in Chapter XIII.

REFERENCES

1.   Statutory Instrument 1962 No.2073, H.M. Stationery Office, price 3d. net.

2.   Statutory Instrument 1959 No.365, H.M. Stationery Office, price 4d. net.

3. G. Livingstone   Research in deafness in children. *Proceedings of a conference*
G. S. Fraser   *organised by the Medical Research Committee of the National Deaf Children's Society*, 1963. London: National Deaf Children's Society. Oxford: Blackwell Scientific Publications.

4. Macleod Yearsley   '*Common diseases of the ear*' London, The Medical Times, 1901. '*The causes leading to educational deafness in children with special reference to prevention*'. London, P. S. King and Son, 1912. British Journal of Children's Diseases, 1934, Vol.31, pp.177 and 272.

Phyllis M. T. Kerridge   Privy Council, Medical Research Council, Reports of the Hearing Committee, '*Hearing and speech in deaf children*', Special Report No.221, H.M. Stationery Office, 1937. '*Defects of hearing in children*', Journal of the Royal Institute of Public Health and Hygiene, December, 1940.

Edith Whetnall   'Deafness in children'; in '*Diseases of the ear, nose and throat*', edited Scott Brown; Butterworth and Co., 1952.

Edith Whetnall   'Causes and pathology of deafness: types of deafness';
and D. B. Fry   Chapter VI of '*The deaf child*'; Heinemann, 1963.

Chapter II. The Context of the Enquiry and the Influence of Educational Aims on Media of Communication

11. We were appointed and have carried out our work at a time of great hopes for the future education of deaf children and substantial achievements existing side by side with disappointment and dissatisfaction. These states of mind are not found uniquely among those concerned with the education of the deaf; they are a characteristic and healthy feature of the contemporary educational scene. Perhaps, however, because the education of deaf children inspires such remarkable devotion and calls upon every resource of ingenuity and intellect, the hopes and disappointment are felt and expressed with particular keenness.

The Education Act, 1944, and subsequent developments

12. The Education Act of 1944 gave legislative form to the principle that the education of handicapped children should be an integral part of the whole education system rather than a self-contained, self-sufficient system governed mainly by considerations not affecting other children. This principle is universally accepted and its application has been accompanied by a great increase and wider dissemination of knowledge of the educational and social handicaps associated with specific disabilities of mind or body and of the measures necessary to overcome or alleviate these.

13. In the education of deaf children, the desire for them to achieve the greatest possible degree of normality has become the more urgent and seemed more capable of fulfilment as advances in medicine and other sciences have opened new fields of educational opportunity. Rapid developments in electronic engineering have brought about a revolution in the design of hearing aids of all kinds, and individual transistor aids are freely available under the National Health Service. Techniques for the early detection of hearing loss, and services organised to discover cases in the infant population, have resulted in a steady increase in the number of children found to have a defect of hearing sufficient to retard their educational progress. Guidance to parents and early treatment and auditory training assisted by the intensive use of amplifying equipment have enabled many more children to be educated as partially hearing who would formerly have been regarded as deaf. The transformation which has taken place is illustrated in Table I and the graph following, compiled from annual returns made to the Department of Education and Science by local education authorities in England and Wales.

Achievements and organisational changes

14. These developments have provided the conditions in which many achievements have been possible. Among the better known are those of the two selective secondary schools, where children have attained high standards in both academic and technical subjects with a remarkable record of success in G.C.E. 'O' and 'A' level examinations; but most other schools can also point to outstanding examples of individual achievement and a general widening of educational and social opportunities for their children. In organisational terms, the major advances made possible by post-war developments were, first, the re-organisation of boarding special schools for children with impaired hearing to provide separately—usually in separate schools but in two special cases in separate

Table I: Pupils with impaired hearing in England and Wales, classified by educational category and type of school attended, 1938-1966

(1) Year	(2) School Population	(3) Deaf Pupils in Special Schools	(4) Rate per 10,000	(5) Partially Hearing pupils in special schools and special classes of ordinary schools	(6) Rate per 10,000	(7) Other school children also provided with hearing aids	(8) Rate per 10,000	(9) Total rate per 10,000
1938	5,053,644	3,585	7·09					
1939 to 1946	NATIONAL STATISTICS WERE NOT COLLECTED DURING THESE YEARS							
1947	5,174,674	2,644	5·10	895	1·73			
1948	5,503,668	3,065	5·56	751	1·36			
1949	5,680,243	3,130	5·51	854	1·50			
1950	5,805,102	3,252	5·60	964	1·66			
1951	5,895,422	3,439	5·83	1,030	1·75			
1952	6,132,334	3,632	5·92	1,093	1·78			
1953	6,373,096	3,816	5·99	1,089	1·71			
1954	6,545,815	3,979	6·00	1,218	1·86			
1955	6,688,840	3,915	5·85	1,295	1·94			
1956	6,824,870	3,894	4·71	1,299	1·90			
1957	6,954,934	3,692	5·31	1,337	1·92	714	1·03	8·26
1958	7,027,156	3,548	5·04	1,357	1·93	1,562	2·22	9·19
1959	7,093,734	3,477	4·90	1,456	2·05	2,127	2·99	9·94
1960	7,123,007	3,463	4·86	1,453	2·04	3,079	4·32	11·22
1961	7,162,125	3,371	4·70	1,480	2·07	3,865	5·40	12·17
1962	7,168,287	3,255	4·54	2,066	2·88	3,925	5·48	12·90
1963	7,133,057	3,016	4·23	2,469	3·46	4,703	6·59	14·28
1964	7,245,501	3,155	4·35	2,567	3·54	4,555	6·29	14·18
1965	7,306,618	3,110	4·25	2,739	3·75	5,243	7·18	15·18
1966	7,400,486	3,048	4·12	2,980	4·03	5,467	7·39	15·54
1967	7,441,600*	2,923	3·93	3,479	4·68	6,006	8·07	16·68

* Approximate

Notes

(a) Column 2 does not include pupils in independent schools.
(b) Column 3: the figure for January, 1938, includes pupils who would now be classified educationally as partially hearing.
(c) Column 5 does not include pupils in special classes before 1962. The first special class for partially hearing pupils at an ordinary school was opened in 1947. Information about the number of such classes in England and Wales was collected for the first time in 1960, followed in 1962 by the first annual return of numbers of pupils in attendance.
(d) Column 7: the figures are calculated from annual returns made for the first time in 1957 of school children provided with hearing aids. The provision of hearing aids under the National Health Service for adults and children began in July, 1948.

8

PUPILS WITH IMPAIRED HEARING IN ENGLAND & WALES

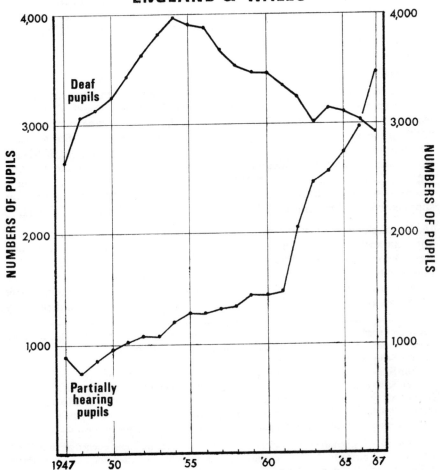

Graph to illustrate the figures in Columns 3 and 5 of Table I.

departments—for the deaf and the partially hearing*; and, secondly, the greatly increased provision of special classes for partially hearing children at ordinary schools†. In addition some local education authorities established peripatetic teaching services for children with impaired hearing not attending special schools‡. Within the special schools the possibility of exploiting opportunities to bring deaf children into more frequent contact with hearing children has not been neglected; many schools, in addition to arranging for children to mix with the hearing on social occasions from time to time, have formed associations with ordinary schools and colleges of further education in order to create new educational openings for their senior pupils. So far as possible residential schools arrange for children to return home at regular intervals during term-time and many are five-day boarders.

The teaching force

15. The recent rapid development of services for pupils with impaired hearing outside special schools has made heavy demands on the supply of qualified teachers of the deaf, i.e. teachers who, in addition to holding qualifications entitling them to the status of qualified teacher, are specially qualified to teach deaf and partially hearing pupils. Between 1959 and 1967, the number of serving teachers in England and Wales with a special qualification to teach the deaf and partially hearing increased from 585 to 816; yet in 1967 the number of these teachers in special schools was 505 as against 521 in 1959. Detailed figures supplied by the Department of Education and Science are given in Table II.

16. Throughout most of the period covered by the table, the total number of pupils in special schools for the deaf and partially hearing (but not in special classes) continued the decline which had started a few years earlier. This fall in numbers has recently begun to level out and it was never sufficient to enable the schools to achieve the levels of staffing they desired. There were in January, 1966, 70 classes out of a total of 533 in special schools for the deaf and partially

---

* Boarding special schools for deaf and partially hearing pupils in England and Wales, *excluding* those for pupils with additional handicaps, are organised as follows:
    (a) Schools admitting only deaf pupils as boarders—16
    (b) Schools admitting only partially hearing pupils as boarders—6
    (c) Schools admitting both deaf and partially hearing pupils as boarders—3
One school in group (c) has recently been re-built and another is being re-built to provide separate teaching and residential accommodation for the two categories of pupils. The third school is one of two selective secondary schools for pupils with impaired hearing.

† Between 1947, when the first special class for partially hearing pupils opened at an ordinary school, and January 1962, when detailed statistics were first collected, the number of classes in England and Wales increased to 66, with 504 pupils in attendance. In January 1967, there were 189 such classes attended by 1,611 pupils. (For both years the figures exclude two groups of special classes attached to ordinary schools. For organisational purposes these classes are regarded as part of nearby special schools for the deaf and partially hearing. There were 13 of these classes in January, 1962, with 114 pupils, and 15 in January 1967, with 124 pupils.)

‡ In January 1967, 66 local education authorities in England and Wales employed peripatetic teachers of the deaf. The duties of these teachers range widely, although not every teacher covers the full range. They include the visiting of young children not yet at school and the guidance of their parents; assistance in the diagnosis and assessment of hearing handicap; and the individual tuition of children with impaired hearing in normal classes of ordinary schools or advising class teachers.

hearing which exceeded the statutory maximum size of 10 pupils prescribed in Regulation 9(a) of the Handicapped Pupils and Special Schools Regulations, 1959[1, 2], the corresponding figures in 1959 having been 98 and 528[3].

Table II: Qualified teachers of the deaf and partially hearing in service in England and Wales, 1959–1966

Number of serving qualified teachers of the deaf and partially hearing (a)	1959	1960	1961	1962	1963	1964	1965	1966	1967
(i) in all special schools (b)	521	531	524	515	542	521	519	510	505
(ii) in special classes	36	50	78	76	88	95	107	140	155
(iii) in peripatetic service	24	24	31	42	69	94	95	105	138
(iv) in local education authority clinics (c)	4	11	11	18	18	10	28	18	18
Total	585	616	644	651	717	720	749	773	816

(a) Some teachers are employed in more than one type of service. This applies more often to teachers in services outside special schools (lines (ii) to (iv)) than to those in special schools. None of these teachers is counted more than once in the table.

(b) i.e. not only in special schools for the deaf and partially hearing.

(c) i.e. excluding hospital and local health authority clinics.

Educational attainments

17. As we previously indicated, advances in educational achievement have been accompanied by an increasingly critical appraisal by teachers and others concerned with the education and welfare of deaf children and adults. The higher attainments of some children have seemed to emphasise the retardation of others. Comparisons are also made between deaf children and children with normal hearing. A recent survey by D. C. Wollman, described in an article published in the British Journal of Educational Psychology in November, 1964, provided additional evidence of the retardation in English and arithmetic of pupils with impaired hearing when compared with un-handicapped pupils[4]. Fears are commonly expressed that the general advance in educational standards is leaving deaf children further behind.

Attainments in speech and lipreading

18. Of major importance to parents of deaf children is the acquisition by tneir children of intelligible speech. Speech attainments were studied in a survey reported in 'The Health of the School Child 1962 and 1963' of 359 children born in 1947 who were in schools for the deaf in 1962 and 1963[5]. The survey included 276 children with a considerable degree of hearing loss, that is to say an average of more than 70 decibels over the speech frequencies. Of these 276 children, excluding 6 who became deaf after the age of five, only 11·6 per cent had clear intelligible speech and good lipreading ability making it relatively easy for the

11

interviewer to communicate with them by speech. Commenting upon ability to communicate through speech, the survey report notes, 'The interview with each child and the intelligence testing of most of them provided an opportunity to assess their ability to communicate with a stranger, either orally or otherwise. It is difficult to assess success or failure in this sort of interview and fine assessment did not in any case seem to be appropriate, so that the children were divided into three broad groups based on speech ability. This is not the only means of communication among deaf children, but it is the means expected of the normal child leaving school and will be expected of the deaf child when he leaves the sheltered environment of school for the less tolerant outside world. Firstly, there were those children with clear, intelligible speech and good lip-reading ability with whom it was quite easy to communicate by speech; secondly, those who had no intelligible speech and thirdly, the majority, with whom it was possible to communicate by the spoken word, but with varying degrees of difficulty and with the help, in some cases, of adjuvant methods of communication. This was usually by writing to augment speech and only as a last resort. . . . It depended very much on the temperament of the individual whether they were seriously discouraged by the interviewer's failure sometimes to understand them at the first attempt; some, used to the far greater ability of their teachers to interpret their imperfect speech, became impatient; others, more withdrawn and less confident, became silent, but most were patient and long-suffering and tried hard and good-humouredly to maintain speech communication'.

Disquiet about results

19. Disquiet about the results of the education of deaf children has been expressed many times by workers among the adult deaf who are conscious of the speech and language deficiencies of members of the deaf community who seek their help and of the inadequate educational attainments of many school leavers coming into their care which impoverish the quality of the social, recreational and working lives of these young people: references to this disquiet were made in the Reports of the Ministry of Education for the years 1960 and 1961. In Chapter II of the Report for 1961[6] the following paragraph appeared:

'The 1960 report referred to the difficulties of those profoundly deaf children who on leaving school have poor educational attainments and speech which often cannot be understood except by their teachers. A further indication of the disquiet which these difficulties cause was evident in the report published during 1961 in professional journals by a group of workers in the spheres of deaf education, welfare and research, which has met informally on a number of occasions to discuss matters affecting the interests of deaf children*. The group thought that it was a matter of first importance that research should be undertaken to investigate what educational provision is needed for children who prove unable to attain an effective capacity to understand and to use spoken language, and to examine the place of manual communication in the education of the deaf. In order to stimulate interest in this problem the group circulated its report among research bodies.'

---

* We understand that the group included members responsible for training teachers of the deaf and for research into problems of deafness in children, head teachers of schools for the deaf, a chief education officer, a consultant otologist, a psychologist and a teacher from a hospital audiology unit, honorary officers of two voluntary societies concerned with the welfare of the deaf, members of H.M. Inspectorate and representatives of the (then) Ministry of Education.

Aims in education

20. This then was the general climate in which we carried out our study. At an early stage it seemed to us that we could not deal adequately with the subject of our inquiry without reference to the aims of educating deaf children and accordingly we paid particular attention to this in taking oral evidence. Without exception the witnesses whose views we sought on this point saw the aims of education as being to fit deaf children so far as possible to take their place in hearing society and to realise a full personal development. Of these witnesses, some placed equal emphasis on preparation for that part of a deaf adult's life which is spent with other deaf people. Societies of the deaf could offer their members substantial cultural, intellectual and social benefits, and the consequences of regarding the deaf community as an inferior sub-culture, an asylum for refugees from the hearing world, were to be deplored. By contrast, there was a body of opinion which believed that the *whole* educational emphasis, except for some of the multiply-handicapped, should be on equipping deaf children to integrate with the hearing world. Since this aim should always be uppermost in the minds of educators, it was incompatible with the use of media of communication not commonly understood by hearing people even if those methods were used only to supplement oral media.

21. In spite of these differing emphases all our witnesses were agreed on the importance for deaf children of proficiency in the use of language, both for personal development and in social and work relationships, whether with the hearing world or with other deaf people. Their differences of opinion arose on the means of achieving proficiency; and their views on this were in turn coloured by their vision of what the future should hold for deaf children. It is arguable that differences of emphasis in aims do not, in themselves, call for widely differing approaches to the question of communication in education; yet it is clear that the extent to which any means of communication is acceptable will continue to vary in accordance with the views held on the place of deaf people in society and with the expectations of parents and teachers for individual deaf children. Among the questions we have asked ourselves is whether factors of this kind should continue to be so influential in educational decisions. Is it the case, in fact, that disparate aims dictate disparate methods? And where aims are shared, can they perhaps be achieved by differing methods? There are teachers of the deaf, here and abroad, who are using finger spelling in an attempt to help young deaf children to speak and lipread and who clearly have the same aim as teachers of the deaf using purely oral methods. Finally, are the aims themselves compatible? There are those who would argue that for some deaf children the aim of integration with the hearing world is incompatible with that of complete personal development.

22. So far, we have discussed general aims and their possible relationship with media of communication used in education. It is also necessary to identify the specific aims or purposes of those who recommend the use of manual media since these may influence both the manner in wnich manual media are used and the stage of their introduction. Broadly speaking, there are four different purposes which finger spelling and signing are considered to serve:

(a) To aid the establishment of oral communication

Those who have this purpose in mind argue that deaf children cannot become competent in oral communication unless they have a sound foundation of language, and that the difficulties of learning to speak, lipread and use

13

residual hearing, if any exists, are so great that oral media cannot of them-selves, even though reinforced by reading and writing, provide an adequate grasp of language. It is necessary, therefore, to use finger spelling or signs, or both, at an early stage to develop language. At a later stage, it is suggested, it may be possible to discard manual media. Within this general purpose, there exists the more limited and specific objective of conveying the structure of spoken words by the temporary use of finger spelling at a very early stage (see paragraph 21). We describe and comment upon this method, as it is practised in the U.S.S.R., in Chapter VII.

(b) To provide substitutes for oral communication

Manual media of communication have been widely used in the past in many countries to teach deaf children to read and write and for their general education. These media were used as a complete substitute for the oral processes by which hearing children learn. Today, very few people would advocate a return to entirely silent methods and those who suggest the use of finger spelling or signs, or both, as a substitute for oral communication assume that oral methods will be tried.

(c) To supplement oral communication

Advocates of manual media of communication in school often recommend their use for this purpose. They point to difficulties which can be resolved by finger spelling key letters which cannot be distinguished in lipreading, to opportunities for accelerating the pace of learning of senior pupils, and to the assistance given by means of an additional visual aid to children who are slow in achieving an adequate level of oral communication. The stage at which a manual supplement should be introduced varies in accordance with the precise purpose for which it is required and as between the individual children for whom it is proposed.

(d) To provide a means of communication in adult life

Finally, there is the objective of providing deaf children with a means of communication with other deaf people in adult life to enlarge their social and educational opportunities within the deaf community. Although those with this objective often appear to accept one or more of the other objectives we have described, some who reject these would still advocate that deaf children, in their last years at school, should be given a command of finger spelling and signing as commonly used among deaf adults.

23. We shall have more to say in later chapters about the aims of those witnesses who commended the use of finger spelling and signs and about the implications of these aims. Our present purpose is simply to indicate the broad distinctions which need to be kept in mind.

REFERENCES

1.   Statistics of Education 1966, Part One, H.M. Stationery Office, price £1 7s. 6d. net.

2.   Statutory Instrument 1959 No. 365, H.M. Stationery Office, price 4d. net.

3.   Education in 1959. Report of the Ministry of Education and Statistics for England and Wales, H.M. Stationery Office, price 14s. 6d. net.

4. D. C. Wollman   *The attainments in English and arithmetic of secondary school pupils with impaired hearing*, British Journal of Educational Psychology, 1964, Vol. XXXIV, Part 3, pp. 268–274.

5.   *Survey of children born in 1947 who were in schools for the deaf in 1962–63*, The Health of the School Child 1962 and 1963, The Report of the Chief Medical Officer of the Department of Education and Science, pp. 60 to 71; H.M. Stationery Office, price 12s. 6d. net.

6.   Education in 1961, Report of the Ministry of Education for England and Wales, p. 24; H.M. Stationery Office, price 8s. 6d. net.

15

Chapter III. The Meaning of Terms

24. Since certain terms which have already appeared in the previous chapters will recur frequently in those which follow, we propose to indicate briefly here the meanings which seem to be most commonly attached to them. Some terms have been used ambiguously in evidence or in the literature, or have had different meanings attached to them by different witnesses. We begin by setting out those which, in our opinion, tend to cause confusion, indicating the alternative meanings which have come to our notice. The meaning corresponding with the definition we have adopted is printed in italics in each case.

Term	Alternative meanings
(i) Oral *	(a) communication which is exclusively oral, unaccompanied by natural gesture; or
	(b) oral communication accompanied by natural gesture and some finger spelling or signing; or
	(c) *oral communication accompanied by natural gesture.*
(ii) Manual	(a) communication which is mainly manual but has some speech added; or
	(b) *communication which is exclusively manual.*
(iii) Combined	(a) a combination of departments within a school in which, for example, the infant department is oral and the remainder of the school uses oral and manual modes of communication together; or
	(b) a mode of communication which is a mixture of signs, finger spelling and speaking; or
	(c) a specific form of combination in which speech is offered continuously and concurrently with manual communication (the "simultaneous method"; see paragraph 13 below) or
	(d) *a generic term to denote a variety of ways of combining oral and manual media.*
(iv) Method	(a) the mode of communication in education; or
	(b) *the way in which communication is taught or established.*
(v) Signing	(a) conventional signing only; or
	(b) gesture; or
	(c) *a generic term referring to the use of signs and gestures of various kinds.*
(vi) Sign language	(a) signing, either (v) (a) (b) or (c); or
	(b) *a system of signs which form a language.*

---

* Confusion is also caused when the term 'purely oral' is used to mean either (i) (a) or (b). In Chapter IX, paragraph 175, we suggest that the general use of the term 'pure oralist', in the sense of (i) (a) is no longer justified.

(vii) Verbal	(a) oral; or
	(b) *concerned with words.*

(viii) Deaf and partially hearing	(a) denoting hearing losses of widely varying degrees within each category, sometimes with overlapping of the categories; or
	(b) *as applied to children, indicating educational category as determined by speech and language development and not by degree of hearing loss.* * *(See Chapter I, paragraphs* 1 *and* 2).

(ix) Impaired hearing	(a) partial loss of hearing; or
	(b) impairment of hearing after the acquisition of speech and language; or
	(c) *any degree of hearing loss including total deafness.* †

(x) Integration	(a) the complete integration of a child or adult with impaired hearing into the hearing community; or
	(b) partial integration; or
	(c) *the degree of integration indicated by the context.*

(xi) 'The deaf'	(a) deaf people with poor language and little or no normal communication; or
	(b) deaf people generally.

(We shall not normally use this term.)

(xii) Oral failure	a deaf child who has made little progress from an oral approach to education.

(We deprecate the use of this term)

25. The remainder of this chapter describes more fully some methods of teaching children with impaired hearing and the various media of communication which may be used for this purpose.

Oral Methods

26. An oral communication is, self-evidently, a communication by word of mouth. It involves the dual ability to speak and to comprehend spoken utterances. Both functions depend primarily upon the sense of hearing and to the extent that hearing is lacking they cannot be performed unless the communicators can rely instead upon the faculties of sight and touch. A child who has little or no useful hearing, even for amplified sound, must be taught how to produce the sounds of speech mechanically if he is to communicate orally. He cannot control the quality, volume or rhythm of sound by hearing his own or

---

* We shall continue to use 'deaf' as a convenient adjective where a precise definition is not required or the meaning is clear from the context; but we shall not apply it to children except in the sense of (viii) (b).

† A view is held that it is misleading to include total deafness within the meaning of this term. While noting this, we find it necessary to have a comprehensive term covering the full range of hearing loss.

17

other voices. To receive and understand the speech of others, he must learn to lipread, that is to perceive what is being said by its appearance on the lips of the speaker. Not all the sounds of speech are visible and some different sounds have an identical appearance. The teaching of these skills and the improvement of techniques for this purpose are important aspects of oral methods of education.

27. Clearly however far more than this is involved since the ability to communicate effectively by word of mouth cannot exist without some command of language. Deprived of the means of acquiring language naturally, or retarded in normal linguistic development, children with impaired hearing, even more than children with normal hearing, need to increase their command of language through reading and writing. Oral education can therefore be described in its basic essentials as the combined teaching of speech, lipreading, reading and writing for the development of language and the acquisition of knowledge through these media of communication.

28. This description, however, omits an important element in current methods, namely the training of residual hearing. Occasionally the term 'oral/aural' is used in preference to 'oral' since it is believed that this indicates more clearly those aspects of modern techniques which are regarded as essential to successful oral education. These are the use of amplified sound to exploit the residual hearing possessed by many children with impaired hearing, including some who would formerly have been regarded as suffering from a total impairment; and the application to auditory training of knowledge of how children with normal hearing learn to speak. Children whose hearing is impaired at birth or soon after need to be given intensive auditory training without delay so that they learn to use any residual hearing they may have to listen not only to other people speaking but also to the sound of their own voice. The first two or three years of life are especially important since these are critical for the normal acquisition of speech and language. We believe that these needs are now generally understood, if not always met, and that when we use the term, oral education, it will be recognised that this includes early auditory training and the continued use throughout school life of amplified sound to supplement lipreading and assist speech training. We shall not therefore generally use the term 'oral/aural'.

29. Readers wishing to study in detail the methods by which children with impaired hearing are taught to communicate orally are referred to the list of books at the end of this chapter.[1] With the exception of two works on the speech and language development of children with normal hearing, included as a source of comparative material, most of the works listed deal mainly with children whose residual hearing can be used in teaching them to speak. 'The Teaching of Speech', by G. Sibley Haycock, describes methods of speech production in children assumed to have no hearing.

Finger Spelling

30. Finger spelling, as its name implies, consists of the spelling out of individual words of the written language, letter by letter, on the fingers, each letter of the alphabet being represented by a particular conventional sign. In this country a two-handed alphabet is in use but many countries, including the United States, use a one-handed alphabet.

Signs

31. There are so many different kinds of signs and varieties of signing that a single definition cannot be attempted. Many of our witnesses distinguished between natural gesture, a movement nearly always understood by a hearing person as by a deaf person, and signing, a system of formalised gestures needing to be learnt like a foreign language. In an analysis in the booklet 'Conversation with the Deaf', published by the Royal National Institute for the Deaf,[2] The Reverend Canon T. H. Sutcliffe identified the following elements in signing:— gesture, used either naturally or in conventional form; facial expression; mime; and the identification of objects by reference to an outstanding characteristic, and of qualities by reference to objects possessing them.

32. In the evidence we received, four main types of signing were described:

(a) The means of communication used among some deaf pupils out of class in which spontaneous gesture often appears to predominate. In general, signing among deaf children at school seems to have developed incidentally from the children's natural gesture often learned from each other, from the signs learned at home by children of deaf parents, and from signs learned by some children visiting clubs for deaf adults.

(b) A means of communication used among deaf adults (often in combination with other means) composed of the elements indicated in paragraph 31.

(c) A systematic sign language with normal grammatical structure, of which the only example reported to us was the language devised by the late Sir Richard Paget and further developed by Lady Paget and Dr. Pierre Gorman, which has been used experimentally with a few deaf adults and children.* A systematic sign language, no longer in use, was created in 1817 by the first Director of the Institute at St. Michielsgestel in Holland, where the school for the deaf now uses purely oral methods. Elsewhere, there have been attempts to standardise the signs used among deaf adults e.g. by eliminating regional variations, and ambiguities. We understand that the College of Deaf Welfare in London has set up a committee, under the chairmanship of the Reverend P. T. Corfmat, which is currently examining the signs in common use to see whether ways can be found to meet some of the criticisms made of them.

(d) Our attention was also drawn to the signs used in combination with finger spelling and speech in the combined department at St. Mary's School for Hearing Impaired Children, Cabra, Dublin. We were informed that this form of signing has a modified linguistic structure in which indications of tense can be given and symbols are available for the different parts of speech.

Combined Methods

33. The term 'combined method' normally refers to any mode of communication where speech and lipreading in varying degrees, with or without amplified sound, are used simultaneously with manual communication.

34. The manual means may be finger spelling alone. This is the so called Rochester method, which was first practised at the Rochester School for the Deaf in New York State. With the one-handed American alphabet and the hand

---

* See paragraph 74.

19

of the speaker held close to the mouth, it is claimed that the listener can watch the hand and lips simultaneously.

35. Another combined method is the Danish system whereby a hand held to the face of the speaker identifies the sounds which are difficult to lipread. Unlike finger spelling, which is a means of representing written words, the mouth-hand system is a means of portraying the phonetic construction of words.

36. Signing is also used, with or without finger spelling, in combined modes of communication. In this case the signs may be used to clarify words that would be ambiguous if reliance were placed on lipreading alone. In the United States of America the term 'simultaneous method' is applied to a combination of media of communication which includes the use of signs. This combination is used at Gallaudet College, Washington D.C., where we understand that it consists of speech, lipreading, the use of hearing aids, signing and finger spelling. The aim is that communication should follow a normal linguistic pattern and we are informed that the articles, conjunctions and verbs are usually finger spelt.

37. A variety of techniques is implied by the term 'combined method' and the differences between them are sometimes of great importance. For example, where both finger spelling and signs are combined with speech and lipreading, there may be a significant difference linguistically between the use of signing to supplement finger spelling and the use of finger spelling to supplement signs. Wherever possible we shall therefore make clear the combination of media to which references are made.

REFERENCES

1. **List of books referred to in paragraph 29**

    Freddy Bloom
    Our Deaf Children (1963), Heinemann

    D. M. C. Dale
    Deaf children at home and at school (1967), University of London Press Ltd.

    I. R. and A. W. G. Ewing
    The Handicap of Deafness (1938), Longmans.
    New Opportunities for Deaf Children (1958), University of London Press.
    Speech and the Deaf Child (1954), Manchester University Press.

    A. W. G. Ewing
    The Modern Educational Treatment of Deafness (1960), Manchester University Press.
    Educational Guidance and the Deaf Child (1957), Manchester University Press.

    A. W. G. and E. C. Ewing
    Teaching Deaf Children to Talk (1964), Manchester University Press.

    M. Greene
    Learning to Talk (A Guide for Parents) 1960, Heinemann Medical.

    Mildred Groht
    Natural Language for Deaf Children (1958), Washington D.C., Volta Bureau, Alexander Graham Bell Association for the Deaf

    Grace Harris
    Language for the pre-school Deaf Child,
    (second edition 1963)   New York, Grune and Stratton.

20

G. Sibley Haycock
The Teaching of Speech (1933), National College of Teachers of the Deaf
(1949), 5th ptg. Washington D.C. Volta Bureau,
Alexander Graham Bell Association for the Deaf.

The Illinois Annual School for Mothers of Deaf Children
If you have a Deaf Child (1951), University of Illinois.

Agnes Lack
The Teaching of Language to Deaf Children (1955), Oxford University Press.

M. M. Lewis
How Children Learn to Speak (1957), Harrap.
Language, Thought and Personality in Infancy and Childhood (1963), Harrap.

Thomas J. Watson
The education of hearing-handicapped children (1967), University of London Press Ltd.

2. T. H. Sutcliffe, "Conversation with the Deaf" (first published 1954; revised 1962, current edition, 1966), Royal National Institute for the Deaf.

Chapter IV. The Linguistic Quality of Methods of Communication

A note on the characteristics of a language

38. Signing, finger spelling and combinations of these are often, we have found, described as 'languages' of the deaf. Whether these media should be called languages depends, it seems to us, on how far they have those essential characteristics of a language which make possible its functions in communication between persons and, for an individual, in relation to his own behaviour.

39. The study today of the nature of a language is notable for its vigorous activity and lively controversy. Here we do no more than consider the criteria of a language by examining the essential characteristics of what would universally be recognised as a language—our own mother tongue.

40. *A definition* commonly accepted is that a language is a system of conventional symbols.

41. *A symbol* is:

(a) a sign made by a person, and

(b) which directs the behaviour of others or of the person himself to a situation,

(c) which may be that in which the sign occurs,

(d) or not actually present when the sign occurs.

42. *The meaning* of a symbol on any one specific occasion is the behaviour evoked—or intended to be evoked—by the symbol on that occasion. (What we call 'the meaning' of a word, e.g. '*the* dictionary meaning' is a collection of specific meanings.)

43. A conventional symbol is a symbol that is not primarily an element of a given situation but is produced in relation to the situation in accordance with the custom of a community.

44. What we have said so far is true of the conventional signing of deaf people. These are symbols by our definitions.

45. A language is a *system* of symbols (not simply a collection of symbols). A mother tongue such as English is a system of verbal symbols, that is, of patterns of vocal sounds or their representation in writing. It is a system in that there is an organisation of grammatical regularities which are regularly related to semantic regularities.

46. The grammatical regularities are in both the accidence and the syntax of a language. Instances of accidence are:

'Noun singular'	ship	dance
'Noun plural'	ships	dances
'Verb, 3rd person singular'	ships	dances
'Verb plural'	ship	dance
'Past tense'	shipped	danced
'Present participle'	shipping	dancing

Instances of syntactical, corresponding to semantic, regularities are: word order, intonation, stress.

47. The highly organised and intricate grammatical and semantic system arises from and serves the needs of human beings in dealing with intricate relationships in individual and social experience. If a new need arises, the regularities make possible the creation of a new symbol which is readily incorporated into the system of the language. The regularities also promote the acquisition of a language.

48. Children with impaired hearing are not only often characteristically defective in their mastery of structure, but, even more notably, tend to be comparatively retarded in the semantic development of their language.

Language and the general development of children

49. Many of our witnesses have emphasised the importance of language not only as a means of communication, but also because it is a permeative influence throughout all aspects of a child's development. Although the specific forms of this relationship are still a subject of controversy, we feel it necessary to attempt an outline of what appears to be its main features.

50. Without doubt, general intellectual, emotional, social and ethical development may occur with a minimum of language; further, it would seem that in some aspects of learning and thinking an undue reliance on words may be a hindrance. There is some evidence that this may occur in the 'concrete' thinking described by Piaget, where the children may be misled by irrelevant verbal associations. There may be important implications here for the education of children with impaired hearing.[1]

51. In children with normal hearing, the main positive functions of language would seem to be to extend the range of experience, to promote more highly-differentiated and discriminative forms of behaviour and to foster regularity and organisation in intellectual and emotional life (cognitive and orectic).* The cognitive and the orectic aspects of development are, of course, closely inter-related and can be considered separately only for convenience in discussion.

52. In *cognitive development* we commonly distinguish such forms of behaviour as perceptual discrimination, conceptual thinking, remembering, imagining, reasoning.

53. For perceptual discrimination there is evidence that for some children as early as the end of the first year the sound of the human voice already tends to attract attention rather more than other auditory stimuli. Observations throughout infancy and childhood suggest that language (including 'internalised' language) helps many children to distinguish finer likenesses and differences in situations of increasing complexity.

54. The beginnings of conceptual thinking, again, are seen in the manner in which children—often within their second year—extend the use of a linguistic response from one situation to another, and subsequently contract its use to a more limited range of situations. In this way the child's linguistic communication with other people influences the classification and organisation of his experiences. For instance, he 'acquires the names of animals'. In general,

---

* Orexis—The motivational and emotional aspects of experience: see J. Drever, Dict. of Psychology, 1952.

it is through language that his conceptual thinking tends to be shaped by the thinking current in the society in which he grows up.

55. In the process of remembering, one of the chief effects of language is to foster accuracy of recall. This is also basically the extension of a specific linguistic form from one situation to another; in this case, from past to present. Normally, in conversation with the child, we reinforce this process. We often encourage him to relate what has happened; by questioning him, and by answering his questions, we help him to recall past events. His remembering becomes increasingly verbalised and so both what he recalls and the organisation of his memory are socially influenced.

56. In similar fashion what we call imagining is at an early stage promoted by language. Imagining seems to begin as an elaboration of remembering and comes to be a recombination and transposition of symbolised past experiences. The symbolisation is freed from its bonds with the past; it may have a reference to the future or be without any time-reference. While imagining may be largely non-linguistic, language may here again promote organisation. In particular, linguistic communication with the child helps to bring his anticipation of the future into relation with his actual past experiences.

57. Finally, when we come to the development of reasoning the importance of language is evident. The child is engaged in attempts to solve problems of increasing complexity and abstractness. The systematic observation of children and experimental work with them, as by Piaget, indicate the successive phases of normal development towards valid formal reasoning and the place of language in each successive phase. In this complex development the child has to achieve a balance between non-linguistic processes and verbalisation. In helping a child to achieve this equilibrium, communication with him becomes a somewhat delicate operation. The intervention of language or an excess of verbalisation may retard his progress.[2]

58. By a child's *orectic development* we mean the progressive organisation of his emotions, the emergence of his personality, the growth of his social life, the differentiation of aesthetic criteria and standards, and the establishment of ethical judgment and conduct.

59. There can be little doubt that all these are closely inter-related and also related to linguistic development. But direct evidence of this latter relationship is even more sparse than in the case of cognitive development and language. Some of the most cogent evidence, indeed, comes indirectly from the study of children whose linguistic development is impaired.

60. We can with some confidence assume that between language and orectic development there is likely to be a constant reciprocal relationship. 'Instability' and 'maladjustment' are likely to retard the acquisition of language; impairment of language, from whatever cause, is likely to retard and distort personal, social and ethical growth.

61. How, then, can language foster the development of a stable and well-adjusted personality? The answer can be given only in general terms. We can look in turn at the various aspects of orectic development and consider how they may be affected by language.

62. On a child's emotional life, language—as emphasised by Russian workers—may have a 'regulatory function'. As a child's emotions are given names, he comes to discriminate them more clearly, to be aware of relationships among them, to organise them into relatively stable patterns and so in a measure to direct and control them. Above all, language may play an important part in stimulating and maintaining a child's motivation to undertake and persist in particular patterns of behaviour.[3]

63. The relationships between language and the growth of self-awareness are even more intricate. The child's acts and the expression of his emotions evoke verbal approval and disapproval from others and so he becomes more clearly aware of his behaviour and attitudes as set beside those of other people. He experiences co-operation and resistance and sees himself as the object of the behaviour of others; language sharpens this awareness. He is helped to see himself as an object of his own behaviour. By becoming aware of his characteristic traits he is more readily able to guide and control his own conduct.

64. The growth and diversification of a child's social relationships are clearly inseparable from his emotional and personal development. Of the three communities in which a child normally grows up—his family, his school and other children—the third is probably the most powerful in fostering his growth towards social maturity. His attitudes and conduct are subjected to a severity of testing and trial as he has to find a way of life with other children. The place of language in his give-and-take has been well brought home to us in the first-hand evidence gathered by I. and P. Opie.

65. Finally, in the ethical development of a child all the effects of language we have mentioned are cumulative. They begin in early infancy as he learns to respond to *No!* and *Yes!* Throughout childhood—in the home, in school and in the playground—these primary verbalisations of prohibition and sanction are expanded and differentiated. Thus, through language, the ethical codes of adults and of other children are brought to bear upon a child's conduct and also upon his judgments of himself and the conduct of others. So in turn his ethical development constantly influences his emotional, personal and social development; the more readily if he is in linguistic communication with others and has some command of inner language.

66. It is evident that the linguistic and general development of individual children with impaired hearing will be influenced by a variety of factors. These we consider in Chapter V.

Media of communication used by deaf people or in the education of deaf children
67. In the infancy of deaf children there is a place for media of communication which are not linguistic for these may assist communication and the general development of the child. In view of the place of language in the general development of children, and bearing in mind the severe linguistic disability inherent in deafness from birth or early infancy, it is nevertheless important that a deaf child should not become habituated to media of communication which are likely to aggravate that disability. Where a medium is intended to promote language it should have those regularities of meaning and structure which are the essential characteristics of a linguistic system.

The effect of the practical limitations of media on their linguistic quality

68. When considering the linguistic quality of each medium of communication which may be used by deaf people, we have to bear in mind not only the primary characteristics of the medium but also its limitations when used with or by the deaf, since these may, in practice, modify it linguistically. For example, speakers vary greatly in their lipreadability and there are certain unalterable physical characteristics and habits of speech which make some virtually unlipreadable. But, even where this does not happen, in the medium itself there are limitations; the appearance of the words seen may be ambiguous or meaningless and the linguistic character of what is said may not be conveyed to the person addressed, even though he may receive the gist of the communication. We shall refer to practical limitations in the following paragraphs where we examine each method of communication.

Oral Media

69. Since the spoken word is the medium of the hearing community its linguistic status is obviously that of the common tongue. If deaf people educated solely by oral media develop imperfect language, the cause must be sought not in the essential character of the medium, but in many extraneous factors, including the difficulties of lipreading to which we have already referred, imperfect understanding arising from the nature of deafness, variations in linguistic ability and other individual differences, and variations in the quality of teaching. These variable factors are discussed in Chapter V. It must also be borne in mind that stress and intonation are absent or only partly present in oral communications received by deaf children and that these lack, therefore, some of the symbolisation of normal spoken language.

Finger spelling

70. As a form of communication the linguistic status of finger spelling is no different from that of the written language and it is capable of use by itself as a completely effective means of communication at a high level among educated deaf adults. This was confirmed by a demonstration which the Reverend Canon T. H. Sutcliffe and Mr. K. Scarratt were good enough to arrange for us, when a complex prose passage, previously unseen by the demonstrators, was finger spelt and translated into written language with complete accuracy. Like oral communication, however, finger spelling may have practical limitations for children or in school. Some of our witnesses have said that there is a tendency to use abbreviations in finger spelling in the classroom, reducing the full notational value of the medium. This would clearly be a practice to guard against if it involved short cuts likely to have an adverse effect on the use and development of language. On the other hand, it appears that finger spelling is sometimes used in an abbreviated form simply to indicate key letters which are ambiguous to the lipreader. Used in this way to clarify speech, abbreviations in finger spelling seem to us not to affect its notational value.*

71. In Chapter VII we describe and comment upon the work in the U.S.S.R. in the use of finger spelling as an initial method of training in the understanding and communication of speech. Observation of deaf children suggests that they

---

* It need hardly be pointed out that the irrationality of English orthography imposes some limitations on this use of finger spelling.

may be less flexible than children with normal hearing in adapting what they have learned to the next stage of learning. It would be necessary to guard against the danger of inflexibility with particular care if finger spelling were used to help young children to acquire language. Reports from the U.S.S.R. suggest that the teaching techniques used there are considered to present no difficulties in the transition from finger spelling to speech.

Signing

72. In Chapter III a number of elements which have been identified in signing are mentioned and we have briefly described the four main types of signing on which we have received evidence. Our witnesses sometimes differed in their views of which elements were dominant but there was general agreement that deaf children signing among themselves out of class, and deaf adults communicating by signs, are both using forms which are ungrammatical and bear little relationship to normal usage. One witness pointed out that where good and fluent signing is used it is not, in fact, a self-sufficient language but parasitic upon well developed mastery of conventional language. In general the assertions were made that in signing as commonly practised by deaf adults the order of signs does not follow normal word sequence, verbs are used less frequently than in the common language and in uninflected form, symbols are lacking for certain parts of speech, and signs sometimes represent words and sometimes ideas, feelings or attitudes. Our evidence is that this form of signing is systematic neither in its structure nor its meanings, although we note that in communication with or between deaf adults it is intended to be used in combination with other forms, mainly speech and finger spelling. We have no reason to doubt that this combination can be an effective means of communication between adults.

73. We also received evidence on the systematic sign language devised by the late Sir Richard Paget and further developed by Lady Paget and Dr. Pierre Gorman. We saw a filmed demonstration of this sign language made in the early stages of its development and studied a manual of the system as it has been developed subsequently. In addition Lady Paget kindly arranged two demonstrations, of which the second took place at a meeting of the full Committee. On that occasion Lady Paget signed a simple prose passage prepared by the Committee which was translated into speech by a teacher of the deaf, who was still a student of the system. The passage contained 100 words from the teacher's known vocabulary of Paget signs; verbs in the past tense were included. It was not seen by the teacher until its transmission by signing. The passage was translated into speech with virtually 100 per cent accuracy, although at a slow pace. In addition, a separate sentence containing a complex verb form 'By Tuesday I will have been walking for two days' was correctly translated into speech, not having been seen in advance.

74. From all the evidence, we are clear that the new Paget systematic sign language follows English syntactical constructions, makes use of accidence and has discrete signs except in the case of synonyms such as 'also' and 'too'. In broad terms, there are generic signs, to which other signs can be added to indicate specific meanings. We are satisfied that the Paget system has the characteristics of a language as defined at the beginning of this Chapter, but we would add that we have at present little evidence of its possible use in the education of children. A pilot study is in progress in Glasgow and we refer to this in Chapter VII.

Combined media

75. The media discussed in the previous paragraphs may sometimes be used in combination and the question arises whether the effect of this is to increase or diminish the linguistic quality of the communication. It was made clear in Chapter III that in oral methods of education in current use deaf children are trained to use what residual hearing they may have, so that they do not have to rely solely on lipreading to understand what is said to them. Research studies have shown that a combination of lipreading and amplified sound leads to more complete reception than is possible when a child has to depend upon one or the other alone. It has also been shown that residual hearing can be exploited most usefully when speech is uttered at a normal pace and with normal rhythm and intonation. In this way a deaf child can get more clues to meaning. As we have said earlier, the symbolic content of the spoken language includes stress and intonation and if these are entirely absent from the experience of a deaf child, his language is inevitably impoverished. If finger spelling is combined with speech, it is possible that it may impose an unnaturally slow pace and artificial rhythm on the spoken word, negating the advantages which would otherwise be gained from residual hearing. Alternatively the normal tempo of speech may be maintained but the finger spelling may not be fully synchronised, thus constituting a distraction preventing the child from making the fullest use of his residual hearing. In the classroom, the teacher who decides to combine these media may have to attend to the problem of their synchronisation. Experimental studies may be needed to investigate the various aspects of this problem.

REFERENCES

1. Instances are in:

E. A. Lunzer, 'Recent Studies . . . . on the work of Piaget', 1960, p.4.

M. M. Lewis, 'Language, Thought and Personality', 1963, p. 179.

H. G. Furth, 'Thinking without Language', 1966, pp. 112, 193.

2. A general discussion of Piaget's work in this connection is offered in:

E. A. Peel, 'The Pupil's Thinking', 1960.

3.

Lewis, 1963, op. cit. 187–9.

Chapter V. Variable Factors likely to affect the Attainments of Children with Impaired Hearing in Language, Lip-reading, Speech and in any of these combined

76. Deaf children, like other children, vary in the standards they attain in spoken and written language. Factors which influence the linguistic development of children with normal hearing also affect that of deaf children but are likely to affect it more critically because of their special defect. Other factors, which have no bearing on the progress of children whose hearing is normal, profoundly influence for good or ill the ability of a deaf child to learn to understand and communicate in his mother tongue. We have listed at the end of this chapter what we consider to be the most important of these factors. We do not suggest that the list is exhaustive.

77. The main factors fall into two broad categories: those which are characteristic of the child and those which occur in his environment. For greater clarity we have sub-divided the environmental factors into three groups, depending upon whether they occur at home, at school, or elsewhere.

78. The following paragraphs provide a commentary on the major items in the list.

Characteristics of the Child

Hearing loss

79. We have previously indicated that the extent and type of a child's hearing loss and the age at which it occurs are major factors influencing his development of speech and language. A child born with a substantial hearing loss or suffering such a loss before the age at which speech and language are normally acquired needs very special attention and treatment at the earliest possible moment. The severity of his linguistic handicap will be aggravated if the impairment of hearing is not discovered at an early stage.

80. When it is suspected that a baby has impaired hearing it is not possible to measure his hearing loss accurately. Instead, a number of simple tests can be used to assess his response to voice and other sounds of different pitch and intensity. When he is a little older, at the age when children with normal hearing begin to respond to spoken language, his capacity for response to this can be tested.

81. Pure tone audiometry is one of the means by which hearing loss may be measured. A pure tone audiometer is an instrument producing sounds, which have no overtones, throughout a range of frequencies and intensities. Intensity of sound is measured in decibels and audiometers are calibrated so that nought decibels represents the threshold of normal hearing. It is thus possible to identify and measure against normal hearing acuity the intensity of sound required before it becomes audible to the person being tested. Since the audiometer can produce tones through a range of frequencies (including those of speech) hearing loss can be measured at the different frequencies and can be plotted as an audiogram.

82. The audiogram of a young child provides useful indications (or confirmation) of the specific difficulties he may encounter in the development of speech

and language through the use of hearing. For example, his hearing loss may be very much greater at some frequencies than at others so that what he hears, even when the sounds are amplified, is distorted. The hearing loss may be greatest in the high frequencies, so that he will have particular difficulty with consonants, which are mainly high frequency sounds.

83. Children with the same pure tone audiograms may vary in their deafness for speech. The techniques used to measure accurately the capacity to hear and understand speech are known as speech audiometry. They make it possible to identify optimum levels of amplification for a child.

84. One reason for variations of this kind as between individuals with similar pure tone audiograms is the factor of progressive impairment of hearing. Of two children with identical pure tone audiograms, one may have had better hearing during the years of normal speech and language development and may be expected to have fewer difficulties in this respect. In other cases, the reason for variations may lie in one or more of the factors enumerated in this chapter.

85. Knowledge of causation is incomplete, and in many individual cases the cause is unknown. But there are certain recognised pre-natal, peri-natal and post-natal causes of deafness which produce characteristic patterns of hearing loss. Where the cause is post-natal, the effect on speech and language development depends upon the child's age at the time of his illness and upon the emotional reaction of the child and his family to the onset of deafness. In some cases this may be extreme, amounting almost to panic.

Use of hearing aid

86. Experience has shown clearly that in all but a few cases, other factors being equal, children deaf from birth or early infancy make better progress if they are fitted in babyhood with suitable hearing aids, prescribed by an otologist, are encouraged to wear the aids continuously and are trained to listen. Naturally, these measures will be helpful only if the aid is kept in good working order and is used in reasonably good acoustic conditions. Some children with severe hearing losses can be helped to discriminate speech and even those who hear relatively little amplified sound and cannot discriminate words may be helped to detect some of the rhythms and other patterns of normal speech and to gain clues to meaning which they would otherwise miss. Comprehension is greater when children combine the use of residual hearing and lip-reading than when either of these methods is used alone.

Additional Handicaps*

87. Some children who are deaf also have other handicaps which affect speech and language development to a greater or lesser degree. Defective sight is an obvious example, affecting a child's ability to lipread. Many other handicaps, such as cerebral palsy and other forms of brain damage, may lead to widely differing attainments in children with the same degree of hearing impairment.

88. Speech and language disorders which may be unrelated to deafness probably occur at least to the same extent among deaf as among hearing children. Many more children with this dual disability are surviving who would formerly have

---

* See also Chapter I, paragraphs 5 to 7.

died at birth and schools for the deaf have an increasing proportion of these pupils.

Intellectual development

89. In Chapter IV we have seen that intellectual development and the development of language are closely connected and interact with each other. Intellectual development is measured by tests of various kinds. In tests which minimise or exclude the use of language so far as possible, the scores of deaf children approximate most closely to those of hearing children.

90. There appears to be some relationship between intelligence and lip-reading ability, but skill in lipreading does not necessarily indicate a high level, or lack of skill a low level, of intellectual ability.

Linguistic aptitude

91. Differences in natural aptitude for speech and for language are known to exist among hearing children and the possibility that such differences also exist among deaf children cannot be excluded.

Personality

92. The personal characteristics of a child may affect his progress in the development of communication. For instance, if a deaf child is to learn to use and understand any method of communication he requires concentration and persistence of a much higher degree than is necessary for a hearing child. Lip-reading cannot be learned or practised unless the lipreader constantly watches the face of the person addressing him. Finger spelling or signing requires a similar degree of concentration on the hands. Whereas hearing may be effective although it is not directed towards a particular source, vision must be narrowly directed and cannot be effective otherwise. To learn to speak at all calls for much effort from a child with a severe hearing loss who finds it difficult to monitor the sound of his own voice; to learn to produce speech which is intelligible to anyone but his teachers, parents and close associates requires him, over many years, to practise patiently and to respond to encouragement, accepting frequent correction. These are heavy demands for any child to meet; they cannot be met so fully by children who are emotionally disturbed or immature or by children in whom distractability or limited powers of concentration are associated with additional handicaps such as brain damage.

Factors in the Home

Socio-economic and cultural factors; size of family and relationships within it

93. The general progress which children with normal hearing make in schools is influenced very considerably by their home circumstances and by their parents' attitudes to education. Their progress in oral and written language depends partly on the quality and quantity of everyday conversation at home, on the kinds of books and newspapers which come into the house, on family habits in reading, watching television and so on, and on parental encouragement to learn. All these factors influence the speech and language development of deaf children as of hearing children.

94. But for deaf children, additional factors or factors which bear upon them with added force have to be taken into account. The demands of a large family may make it difficult or impossible for the mother of a young deaf child to give him the individual attention he needs. It is obvious that, even more than a hearing child, a deaf child requires the constant attention of his mother in the early years. His relationship with other members of the family may also influence his progress in speech and language. If brothers and sisters with normal hearing understand his difficulties, their presence may help him to learn to talk. The physical conditions of the home are also relevant; any living conditions making it more difficult for a deaf child to see or hear aggravate the situation.

Deafness in the family
95. The parents of some deaf children are themselves deaf and in some of these families the main media of communication may not be oral. Special measures are usually needed to ensure that the early development of the children's speech is not retarded. On the other hand, many skilled observers maintain that the subsequent development of speech and language is helped by the fact that the children from an early age have had good communication within their families.

The guidance of parents
96. As we have indicated in Chapter II, help and guidance to those with whom a deaf child grows up are critical factors in the development of his speech and language. Although not available everywhere, services are now provided in many areas to help parents of young deaf children to understand and accept their child's handicap, to guide them in his training at home and in their development of a positive attitude to this, and to continue to give them guidance and encouragment, if necessary, while he is at school. It is evident, however, that differences are bound to persist in the willingness or ability of parents to co-operate with these services.*

Factors in the School

Types of special educational treatment
97. Arrangements for the education of children with impaired hearing range from attendance at an ordinary day school, with or without assistance from a teacher of the deaf, to the provision of boarding education in a special school for the deaf. Severity of educational handicap as defined in Chapter I is obviously a major factor in decisions taken about the placement of individual children, but the availability and character of local services and the wishes of parents in such matters as boarding education also have to be taken into account. So it happens that some children whose degrees of handicap seem very similar may be found in different educational environments which may influence in different ways their progress in speech and language. To take one example, a child in a special class for partially hearing pupils at an ordinary school may benefit from frequent association with children whose speech and language are normal and his progress in these respects may be greater than that of a similar child placed at a special school. On the other hand, he may prove to be a child for whom this

---

* A study of the respective effects of provision and lack of adequate provision of pre-school training and guidance is briefly described in paragraph 206.

regime is too demanding. Unable to benefit from joining the activities of the children with normal hearing, he may have fewer opportunities for developing speech and language than would have been available to him in the larger group of handicapped pupils in a special school.

Size and composition of schools

98. Within the special schools, there are considerable variations in size of school and age-range of pupils. These are illustrated in Table III, compiled from information supplied by the Department of Education and Science. In some small schools, catering for a wide age-range, classification of pupils is difficult and groups may be mixed in age, ability and severity of handicap. A child with good potentiality for speech and language may not be able to realise this fully in a group of children whose capacity is more limited.

Table III   Special Schools for the Deaf and Partially Hearing in England and Wales, Analysed by Type, Age Range and Size

Type of School	Age range	Number of Schools with a roll of					Total Schools
		0–49	50–99	100–149	150–199	200 and over	
Day schools for the deaf	2–12	2	2				4
	Below 5–16		2	2			4
	12–16	1					1
Day schools for the deaf and partially hearing	Below 5–16		7	2	2		11
	5–16	1					1
Boarding schools for the deaf	2– 7	1					1
	Below 5–12	1	1				2
	Below 5–16		2	4	3	2	11
	12–16		1				1
	11–19	1					1
Boarding schools for the deaf and partially hearing	Below 5–16	1		1	1		3
	8–16	1					1
	11–19				1		1
Boarding schools for the partially hearing	Below 5–16			4			4
	7–16		1	1			2
	9–16		1(a)				1
Total Schools		9	17	14	7	2	49

Notes: (a) This school is being reorganised progressively to provide for an age range of 12–16.

(b) At schools where the upper age limit is given as 16 children may stay beyond this age.

33

Staffing

99. Staffing ratios in special schools and the stability of staffing also vary. In schools of all kinds there is often considerable movement of staff but a deaf child in this situation, taught by a succession of teachers, may be confused by their differing practices and ability to be lipread and may suffer more than a hearing child from unevenness in the quality of teaching. Information on staff changes in special schools for the deaf and partially hearing is given in 'Units for Partially Hearing Children, Education Survey 1'[1], where the results of a special enquiry are reported. This showed 603 full-time teachers in post in November, 1966, in 47 special schools for the deaf and partially hearing. (We understand that this number included 137 teachers* not qualified to teach the deaf: see paragraph 100 below.) In these schools in the previous five years there had been 553 staff changes for all reasons.

100. All special schools for the deaf and partially hearing have on their staffs at one time or another a proportion of teachers not qualified to teach children with impaired hearing. This is because teachers are allowed to teach in these schools for up to three years before obtaining a special qualification, and teachers engaged in the teaching of craft or domestic subjects are not required to obtain a special qualification as a condition of continued employment in special schools for the deaf and partially hearing. Table IV supplied by the Department of Education and Science from annual returns made by special schools for the deaf and partially hearing shows the number of teachers without a special qualification to teach the deaf who were employed in each of the last eleven years.

Table IV Numbers of Teachers Not Qualified to Teach the Deaf in Special Schools for the Deaf and Partially Hearing in England and Wales, 1957 to 1966

January	1957	1958	1959	1960	1961	1962	1963	1964	1965	1966	1967
	127	99	99	113	111	136	134	172	132	142	191

We understand that the enquiry conducted in 1966 showed that only a small minority of these teachers would be able to continue in post without obtaining a special qualification to teach deaf children.

School policies and practices

101. Schools also vary in their policies, some placing greater emphasis than others on e.g. the direct teaching of speech and language or on the use of a wide range of amplifying equipment and other teaching aids. In boarding schools, the day-by-day application of policy on communication depends not only upon teachers but also upon house-staff, with whom children may spend much of their time. In some areas, the recruitment and training of house-staff presents many problems and children may be exposed to media of communication which would be unacceptable in other schools, or the nature of their linguistic difficulties may not be fully understood. The present practices of schools in methods of communication are described in Chapter VI. Appendix B gives figures showing the extent to which natural gestures, signs and finger spelling are used by child care

---

* These 137 teachers were in 47 schools. The figure of 142 in the 1966 column of Table IV relates to 48 schools. The collection of the figures in different months of the year may have caused a further discrepancy.

staff communicating with children, and between children both in and out of class (see next paragraph).

Media of communication among pupils

102. There are also variations between schools in the media of communication used among children. Some schools insist on the use of speech, lipreading and amplified sound at every opportunity; others take the view that children's freedom of expression should not be curbed when they are communicating with each other. Signs and gestures are commonly used outside the clasroom; these are passed on by one generation of pupils to another and are sometimes traditional within the school.

Factors Outside School and Home

Relationships with adults and with other children

103. Children are influenced, especially as they grow older, by the relationships they form outside the immediate circle of home and school. Children with impaired hearing who are understood and accepted by hearing friends and neighbours and whose social life can be extended to include interests open to the hearing are likely to have richer and more varied experiences of life from which knowledge of language can be enlarged. A similar enrichment may follow from contact and communication with other people with impaired hearing. Opportunities and the ability to enjoy this breadth of experience vary not only as between children and families but as between one town and another and the town and countryside.

Conclusion

104. We have had two considerations in mind in describing in some detail the major variable factors likely to affect linguistic attainment in children with impaired hearing. First, it has sometimes been implied that failure in any aspect of linguistic development can be attributed to a single cause and is likely therefore to be amenable to a simple cure. If this were the case our task would be relatively easy; in fact the evidence we have received shows that the causes of success or failure are complex and variable. Secondly, by setting out the factors which may be responsible for failure in individual cases it is possible to identify those for which amelioration may be attempted and those which cannot be controlled or altered.

105. Any attempt to consider the possibilities of different means of communication in the education of deaf children must bear in mind this range of factors which influence a child's progress.

REFERENCE

1. *Units for Partially Hearing Children, Education Survey 1*, Department of Education and Science, pp. 27, 28; H.M. Stationery Office, 1967.

Variable Factors likely to affect the Attainments of Children with Impaired Hearing in Language, Lipreading, Speech and In any of these combined

I. Characteristics of the child

1. Hearing impairment (a) degree
                         (b) causes
                         (c) age at onset
                         (d) age at ascertainment
                         (e) changes in degree of hearing loss, if known.
2. Use of hearing aid
    (a) Nature and frequency of use of hearing aid, if any
    (b) Effects, if any, of use of hearing aids.
3. Handicaps other than deafness.
4. Intellectual development.
5. Possibility of differences in linguistic aptitudes.
6. Personality: emotional adjustment, powers of concentration, distractability, hyperactivity.

II. Factors in the home

7. Socio-economic level and conditions affecting education.
8. Deafness in immediate family and among relations.
9. Parents' attitudes and practices in child-rearing, and relationship with child.
10. Relationships with siblings.
11. Size of family.
12. Guidance and encouragement given to parents before and during child's schooling, and their response to these.
13. Media of communication.

III. Factors in the school

14. Type and size of school e.g. partially hearing unit or day special school, ratio of adults to children.
15. Range of 'educational deafness' among children.
16. Child's school history, including continuity of teaching and stability of staffing.
17. General school policy and principles of education; trained attitudes of house-staff; school equipment and its use.
18. Media of communication with adults.
19. Media of communication among children.
20. Quality of teaching.

IV. Factors outside home and school

21. Relationships with other children.
22. Relationships with adults.

Chapter VI. Present Practices in the United Kingdom and the Republic of Eire

106. Our enquiry is concerned with the education of deaf children in England and Wales, but we have also made some study of practice in other countries, including the rest of the United Kingdom and the Republic of Eire. In this we have been greatly assisted by the Scottish Education Department and Scottish schools, and by head teachers of schools for the deaf in Northern Ireland and Eire.

England, Wales and Scotland

107. In schools for the deaf, as in all other schools, central government does not interfere with the discretion of teachers to use whatever methods they consider to be the most helpful to children's development. A school however is not insulated from external influences, and the views and practices of teachers of the deaf, inevitably and properly, are shaped or modified by many currents of thought. Among the possible influences are the wishes of parents for their children's future, the nature of the professional training received by intending teachers, the corporate views of teachers as a professional body, and the opinions of former pupils and those who speak on their behalf.

108. We shall describe in detail in later chapters the evidence given to us by individuals and organisations representing these points of view. It is sufficient to say here that most of the formative influences in the education of deaf children for many years have been directed to the development of oral methods and the professional training of teachers of the deaf is concerned with teaching methods which are exclusively oral. It is not surprising therefore that a view persists that the great majority of schools for the deaf adhere scrupulously to the use of purely oral methods. Yet there are indications in the evidence we have received that this view is not entirely justified; the impact of other points of view on the practice of individual schools and teachers can be clearly recognised. There are schools where some use is made of manual media of communication to assist backward children, to impart information more quickly to senior pupils, to overcome ambiguities in lipreading, and even in one case to experiment in the teaching of language to young children by the supplementary use of finger spelling.

109. The evidence we received from individual teachers was not in itself, however, sufficient to enable us to assess the extent to which schools were either deliberately introducing the use of manual methods in teaching or permitting their use out of school hours. We therefore devised a simple questionnaire (reproduced in Appendix B) which was sent to all special schools and independent schools for pupils with impaired hearing and all special classes for partially hearing pupils at ordinary schools in England and Wales. With the co-operation of the Scottish Education Department the questionnaire was also sent to comparable schools and classes in Scotland.

110. Schools were invited to complete the returns anonymously and to fill in a separate copy of the questionnaire for each of the stages of education, nursery and infant, junior or secondary with which they were concerned. Returns were

received from 50 schools and 96 units* in England and Wales, compared with a maximum possible at the relevant time of 54 schools and 111 units. The returns received covered 4,262 children at schools, plus the numbers at four schools which omitted to enter their numbers on roll, and 1,033 children in units, plus the numbers at 3 units which also failed to enter numbers on roll. From Scotland, returns were received from 10 schools and two units, covering 675 and 19 children respectively.

111. The full replies are summarised in Appendix B, which also contains a table showing the number and type of schools where signs and finger spelling are used by teachers to children. Table V below, which takes all the returns from schools for the deaf, or deaf and partially hearing, from England, Wales and Scotland together, indicates the percentages of the schools in these categories responding which make no use, some use, or frequent use of manual media in the classroom at the various stages. A positive return from a school might indicate occasional use with a small number of children; we did not consider it practicable to ask schools to estimate the extent of the use of these media.

Table V—Schools for children with impaired hearing

Percentages of schools responding (excluding schools and units for partially hearing pupils only) which never, sometimes or often use manual media of communication in teaching

	Never	Sometimes	Often
Finger Spelling			
Nursery and infant	91%	9%	
Junior	63%	37%	
Secondary	49%	40%	11%
Signing			
Nursery and infant	85%	15%	
Junior	80%	18%	2%
Secondary	67%	29%	4%

The proportion of schools making some use of manual media by the secondary stage is clear from this table.

112. Some of the schools volunteered information about the circumstances in which teachers use manual media of communication in class. The circumstances mentioned included the following:—

Children not developing well orally, from one cause or another.
With dull children.
With children with brain damage or severe language disorders.
With children with cerebral palsy.
With maladjusted children.
With dually handicapped children.
With children of deaf parents.
With immigrant children.
With children transferred from other schools.

---

* In this context, the term 'unit' means a special class or group of special classes for partially hearing pupils at an ordinary school. In effect, the number of units represents the number of ordinary schools involved.

Manual media used in order to impart information quickly (at secondary stage chiefly).

Manual media used in order to satisfy children's need for expression.

Experimental use of finger spelling to help young children to speak and lipread.

113. Children may often use signs when it is not the school's intention that they should do so. Some schools commented upon this, giving instances as follows:—

Children with deaf parents, relatives or friends at home.

Children transferred from residential schools for the deaf.

Children who started late at school.

Children suffering from damage to the central nervous system.

Immigrant children.

Children who have learned signs from older children.

Profoundly deaf children.

114. A number of additional comments were received and these are summarised in the following paragraphs:

Use of manual media in combination with oral media

115. Seven schools and one partially hearing unit indicated that where gesture, finger spelling or signing was used by a child they would expect it to be accompanied by an attempt at speech. One school mentioned unvoiced speech accompanying signs in child to child communication.

Prohibitions or discouragements

116. Six comments were made indicating that schools actively discouraged or disapproved of signing. Two of these comments were applied also to finger spelling. One school commented that parents of deaf pupils resented signing to their children. One partially hearing unit commented that any question of finger spelling and signing did not arise with them; in this connection we noted the omission of both positive and negative entries in the 'finger spelling' and 'signs' lines of the questionnaire by partially hearing units to a greater extent than by schools.

Knowledge of manual media by staff

117. Where the replies to the questionnaire stated that use is made, sometimes or often, of finger spelling or signing, by children to teachers, by teachers to children or by children to child care staff, there is obviously a clear indication that the staff concerned have some knowledge of these media. We have, however, no evidence to enable us to estimate the extent of this knowledge, and we did not find it practicable to attempt to ascertain the number of these teachers or the extent of their knowledge.

Use of finger spelling at the Nursery/Infant Stage

118. In addition to questions about the use of finger spelling and signs, schools were asked whether they used natural gesture. In general the returns and special notes indicated that natural gesture, mime, dramatisation, are far more commonly used at the nursery/infant stage than finger spelling, but there was a small number of cases where finger spelling was shown to be used at this stage.

One school began in April, 1965, an experiment with the use of lipreading combined with the one-handed finger spelled alphabet.

119. The special notes offered little detailed information on the methods and policies of the small number of schools who use finger spelling at the nursery/infant stage, but some indications were given. Of the two boarding schools for the deaf who use finger spelling with nursery or infant children, one said that this was due to the high proportion of children with dual handicaps, with whom non-oral methods were essential if contact was to be established. They did, however, maintain an oral approach so far as possible. The other school indicated that the use of finger spelling occurred only with the older infants. Notes written by other schools who did not use finger spelling at the nursery/infant stage, indicated that with their youngest children they aim to develop hearing and speech to the greatest extent of which the children are capable. Two schools added however that it was not their aim to restrict freedom of expression, and one of these schools said that no disapproval was shown when a child offered communication by non-oral means. The point was made more than once that young children do not know finger spelling or a developed system of signs unless they have deaf parents, relatives or friends from whom they have learned them. It may be, therefore, that schools who said they sometimes use finger spelling with children at the nursery/infant stage, and gave no further explanation of what is involved, meant that they use it with one or two children who happen to know the alphabet and with whom they think it will be helpful.

Northern Ireland

120. Current practice at Jordanstown School, the only school for the deaf in Northern Ireland, was described to us by the principal. This school caters for deaf and partially hearing pupils in separate departments; half the children in the school are resident and half attend by day. At the senior stage, deaf children with good oral ability are placed in the partially hearing department. For other senior deaf pupils (in 1965/66 they numbered 25, as against four pupils transferred to the partially hearing department) finger spelling is used in class as an adjunct to the amplified spoken word whenever this is necessary to maintain the pace of learning. In practice, finger spelling needs to be used only for the occasional word to avoid confusion arising from lipreading. Among the pupils helped in this way are some of dull intelligence and some whose deafness was discovered late or special schooling delayed. Deaf children with additional handicaps are placed in a diagnostic teaching unit where a variety of methods is being developed experimentally.

The Republic of Eire

121. The principals of the two main schools for the deaf in the Republic of Eire also gave us information about current practice at their schools.

122. St. Mary's School for Hearing Impaired Children, Cabra, Dublin, was a silent school until 1946 when oral methods were introduced. It caters for deaf and partially hearing girls from Eire and is now organised in separate deaf and partially hearing departments, both using purely oral methods, and in a third separate department where a combined medium of communication is used. Out of a total roll of 250 pupils, only about 20 are in the combined department, to which pupils are not normally admitted until they have passed the age of seven

years. The pupils transferred to the combined department are those who have failed to make progress by oral methods and are mostly children with additional disabilities or children whose special schooling was delayed. The medium of communication used in teaching these children is the system of signs combined with speech and finger spelling referred to in paragraph 32(d). The role of finger spelling in this combined medium is simply to make good deficiencies in the vocabulary of signs.

123. St. Joseph's School for Deaf Boys, Cabra, caters for deaf and partially hearing boys from all parts of Eire. Every child admitted to the school begins with oral methods of education, normally at the age of four or five years. If, after two or three years, it is apparent that a child is not making satisfactory progress, a change is made to manual media of communication, subject to parental consent; but wherever possible these media are combined with speech and lip-reading.

Conclusion

124. This review has demonstrated that considerable variations exist in the media of communication used in the education of deaf children in the United Kingdom and Eire; and it has established that, although there are schools which actively discourage or disapprove of manual media, a substantial proportion makes some use of these media. In the absence of a comparable review at an earlier period it is impossible to be certain how far the enquiry has brought to light long standing practices not generally known to exist and how far it reveals a changing pattern. It has shown some aspects of the situation as it exists now, but any further interpretation of the results must be approached with caution. More detailed questions of the practice in schools may need to be investigated and we deal with this in Chapter XIII.

Chapter VII. Theory and Practice in some Foreign Countries, with Notes on Research and Experiment in the United Kingdom and Overseas

125. Although we could not make a comprehensive study of theory and practice abroad we took note of major aspects of practice in a number of countries other than England and Wales*, paying special attention to recent changes which seemed to have a bearing on our enquiry. In this part of our work we were greatly assisted by Mr. H. G. Williams, a member of H.M. Inspectorate of Schools, who carried out for us a survey of relevant foreign literature and research papers.

126. Most of the relevant research and experimental work, so far as we could discover, is being carried out overseas. There are however two recent pieces of work in Scotland, one of which is still in progress, which are referred to in the final section of this chapter.

127. The changes of practice which we now describe refer to movements towards both a greater and a lesser use of oral media of communication in teaching. It should be noted however that although those responsible for introducing these changes were setting out in different directions from different starting points they all hoped to arrive at the same destination—a state of improved oral proficiency and linguistic development of deaf children.

Recent changes in practice

(i) *The use of finger spelling in the education of deaf children in the U.S.S.R.*
128. The following account is based on the mainly Russian papers listed at the end of this chapter[1], on other papers referred to in the text and also listed, and on a report submitted to us by the Principal Medical Officer of the Department of Education and Science and the Under Secretary in charge of the Department's Special Services Branch who visited the U.S.S.R. for two weeks in 1966 to see and learn something of the Russian method of teaching young deaf children.

129. Until about 1950, oral methods predominated in the education of deaf children in the U.S.S.R., and the main emphasis was placed on speech training. Neither individual hearing aids nor other means of amplification were in use. Understanding of speech was inculcated through lipreading, though reading was also utilized by means of 'flash cards' on which words were written. But these techniques were found to be ineffectual in that children did not learn to understand or enunciate more than a few words and phrases, and these only vaguely and inaccurately. After much discussion it was decided to employ finger spelling (dactylography) as an initial method of training in the understanding and communication of speech; and to introduce it as early as possible, at the age of 3-4 years, in kindergartens and nursery schools. At first the method was employed only in the experimental kindergarten of the Institute of Defectology in Moscow. Its use was gradually extended to other schools (20 by 1958) and by 1960 it appeared to the Institute to be established that the method was more successful than the oral methods previously in use. It became official

---

* See Chapter VI

42

policy to adopt the new method throughout Russia and to use it in all kinder-gartens for deaf children (aged about three to six years), in all other schools for the deaf, and with deaf children of school age (seven years) who had not previously attended a kindergarten. It is not used in the separate schools for the hard of hearing*. Various experiments have been described which are claimed to prove that the Russian method produces better results than did the previous oral training. For reasons given below, we would suggest that this experimental evidence should be accepted with caution.

130. The superiority of finger spelling in the early stages of learning to speak and understand speech is attributed to its accuracy and clarity in conveying the exact structure of words. Within 30-40 days children learn the finger signs corresponding to phonemes. Thereafter, the teacher must at all times enunciate the words exactly in time with their finger spelling, with the hand held immediately below the chin, in order that the children may learn to associate the finger spelt patterns with the visual patterns perceived in lipreading. The children must also attempt to enunciate words while finger spelling them. But in order to obtain a close integration between finger spelling and oral articulation, these must be practised together from the beginning. It is claimed that electromyograph records show that in children taught thus, articulatory and finger muscle movements are in fact closely integrated. As soon as possible, written words are introduced; these are shown to the children on 'flash cards' and the children are required to write them themselves.

131. It is emphasized that the words used should always relate to the children's own experiences and their familiar activities. In this way, they learn to understand a considerable vocabulary during the early years of training. Some figures were given at the First International Conference of the Association for Special Education in 1966, where a speaker from the U.S.S.R. reported that deaf children entering kindergarten at different ages have different vocabulary levels, both in volume and quality, after one year of learning. Children aged two years accumulate up to 86 words, aged three years up to 448 words, aged four years up to 472 words and aged five years up to about 500 words. Children aged five years who have been learning for three years have an average of 1000 to 2000 words, have mastered grammatical generalisations and elementary narrating and use in their speech 70% of all mastered words[2].

132. It is claimed also that children lipread no worse, and sometimes better, than children trained orally throughout. When their own speech develops in association with finger spelling, enunciation is smoother and more accurate than in orally trained children. A further advantage of finger spelling is that it inhibits the unsystematic signing which children tend to use spontaneously in their attempts to communicate with each other. After a time, lipreading is

---

* We understand that children are initially allocated to schools for the deaf or hard of hearing on the basis of speech development and not on their hearing loss. If a child with defective hearing has no speech he is classified as deaf. Most children classified as hard of hearing have a maximum hearing loss of 65–70 decibels (very rarely up to 75 db.), but the loss must not be greater than 60 db. at frequencies 1000 and 2000. Individual hearing aids are not available and no attempt is made to exploit residual hearing in very young children. An unknown number without speech must therefore come forward for testing at the age of about three (when testing begins), or over, who are classified as deaf but who would, in this country, have at least a little speech and initially be classified as partially hearing.

practised without finger spelling; and there should also be systematic drill in enunciation. It is claimed that by the end of the first year of training, children are beginning to give up finger spelling in speaking, and spontaneous vocalization develops. Finger spelling remains necessary only in helping children with new and unfamiliar words.

133. It is stated that an important feature of the method is that it is based in the early stages on an abbreviated phoneme system. In this 'concentric method', as it is termed, a maximum of 17 basic sounds is used from the 42 phonemes of the Russian language. Initially, children are allowed, when attempting speech, to substitute one phoneme for another similar one within prescribed limits in which kindred sounds, such as 'p' and 'b', are grouped. The aim is to avoid confusion between the groups; later, discrimination within each group is introduced. A detailed description of the use of the concentric method is given in a paper by Manfred Greulich in 'Neue Blätter fur Taubstummenbildung', Heidelberg, 1965[3]. This article also describes in detail the transition from finger spelling to speech.

134. Certain comments are relevant to the interpretation of the results of these experiments. Russian orthography is highly phonemic and there is therefore a closer natural correspondence between spoken and finger spelt words than in English. It does not appear from the literature that, in the experiments performed, the efficacy of oral methods with and without finger spelling was compared by using matched groups of children taught simultaneously. In so far as the performance of children taught purely orally was compared with that of children taught with the aid of finger spelling at a later period, other factors, for instance, general improvements in educational method, may have favoured the latter*. Furthermore, it is clear that the association of manual techniques with oral training was considered to be in line with Pavlov's principles of conditioning. As a result, they were accepted and operated with enthusiasm, which again would have tended to promote favourable results.

135. The officers of the Department of Education and Science who were able to observe children at work in a kindergarten and two schools for the deaf in Moscow included in their report the following account of their observations, which were made during normal school days and not at specially arranged demonstrations:

'The children of four, five and six years old whom we saw in class certainly understood their teacher well, and mostly spoke freely and often with good voice, although they were regarded as being profoundly deaf and were unselected groups. We could not judge the intelligibility of the speech, but our interpreter (who had never previously seen a deaf child) said that she could understand some of them. The children were also very lively and spontaneous, and did not appear to be oppressed by the methods used, which might strike someone accustomed to English methods as unsuitable for young children.

---

*The experimental stages from 1952–1960 were however concurrent with a continued use of purely oral methods in the non-experimental schools and it seems probable that a comparison of results during the period in question was a factor in the recommendation made in 1960 by the Institute of Defectology that the method should be generally adopted.

The same was true of the two deaf schools we visited—the experimental school at the Institute of Defectology and the largest and most modern deaf school in Moscow, both having a compulsory age range of 7-16, with most pupils staying to 19. In these schools we saw classes at various ages, and here too communication was very free and lively, both between the pupils and with the teacher, reliance being placed very largely on lipreading; the children also used finger spelling themselves, with speech, but the teacher only for the occasional word. There was no amplification, nor were there any individual hearing aids in any class in either school. Our interpreter understood many children in the middle and upper school, but she found the speech of the seven year old class (who had not previously attended a kindergarten) unintelligible.'

136. Although the officers of the Department of Education and Science found that the Russians made less use than is made in this country of hearing aids and consequently of the exploitation as an educational medium of residual hearing, and also did not apply screening tests to very young children, they commented as follows:

'It appeared to us, from what we were shown, that the Russians are more successful than we are in the development of language, vocabulary and speech in deaf children once they enter the educational system. This seemed to us to be a strong point in favour of their method (use of finger spelling from the very start as an instrument for the development of language, communication and speech), the investigation of which was the main object of our visit.'

137. An article describing former and present methods of educating deaf children in the U.S.S.R. was published by H. G. Williams in The Teacher of the Deaf, 1960[4]. To this article is appended a paper by B. V. Morkovin, Experiment in teaching deaf pre-school children in the Soviet Union, Volta Review, 1960[1(i)]. The list of mainly Russian papers given at the end of this chapter,[1(a) to (v)], includes manuals which specify the exact procedures and materials to be used by Russian teachers of deaf children.

(ii) *Changes in practice elsewhere*

138. Developments elsewhere leading to the general adoption of new methods seem to be relatively few and to be mainly in the direction of a more intensive use of oral media or their adoption for the first time. We have previously mentioned (paragraph 122) that St. Mary's School for Hearing Impaired Children, Cabra, Dublin, *Eire*, was a silent school until 1946. In that year the school changed to oral methods and these have since been used exclusively in the education of the majority of pupils attending the school. At the same time, speech, lipreading and amplified sound were added to the signs and finger spelling used to teach the small number of pupils who were found still to need the help of manual media of communication. The Principal told us that experience in the years immediately after the change to oral methods suggested that children who were being taught by these methods exclusively did not make adequate progress while they continued to associate with children using manual media or if they were permitted to use signs outside school hours. This experience led to a policy of separation which was applied both in and out of class.

139. In *Italy*, there appear to be new trends in the direction of early auditory training and the guidance of parents of young children with impaired hearing. The system of auditory training initiated by Professor Adelaide Grisoni-Colli at the clinic of the Child Neurology Department of The Instituto Neurologico 'Carlo Besta', Milan, is described by her in a paper published in this country in 1964[5].

140. A different point of view was represented in an article published in Italy in the previous year[6]. This recommended the use of finger spelling as an aid in the teaching of speech. Among the reasons given were the assistance finger spelling is said to offer where difficulties occur in lipreading and its possible role as a deterrent to the use of signing, cf paragraph 132.

141. In paragraph 32(c) we mentioned the systematic sign language formerly used at the Institute at St. Michielsgestel in *Holland*. Although its use was abandoned during the second half of the 19th century, a system involving a combination of the signs with speech was tried during 1939–46. This experiment is described briefly in an article published in The Teacher of the Deaf, April, 1960, in the following terms '. . . . . a system that involved a combination of van Beek's signs with speech, for three and four-year-old pupils, was discussed and tried on feeble-minded deaf persons. The aural-oral approach, begun in 1946, has proved a better approach to literacy, even for feeble-minded deaf children. Even children whose hearing losses exceed 90 decibels have experienced, through using hearing aids in combination with lipreading and through auditory training, the rhythm of spoken language which modern studies emphasise as one of its essential features.'[7]

Established practices and indications of dissent

142. In continental *Europe*, practice varies from one country to another. Within most countries, as in the United Kingdom, there appears to have become established a single main tradition, but the literature suggests the existence of individual differences of view and practice.

143. In the *German Federal Republic* oral methods have predominated for many years but some thought is being given to the use of signs as a means of developing language. A work published in 1964 describes a key devised by the author which employs signs in addition to other visual means, like colour and positions, to teach sentence structures. It is suggested that all deaf children have an inner capacity for language which must be developed from an early age by a means which prevents their natural gesturing from degenerating into an esoteric system[8].

144. A different approach is being adopted empirically in a school in Berlin, where the Danish mouth-hand system* is currently in use. In a direct communication from the director of senior studies at the school for the deaf at Charlottenburg, Berlin, we were informed that the Danish mouth-hand system has been used for the past five years with a class of children whose use of the system began when they were four years old. As their oral ability has increased the children have gradually dispensed with the hand signs with which they accompanied their speech. Similarly, their teacher now uses few hand signs in presenting known material, reserving the mouth-hand system for the introduction of difficult new terms and for the correction of speech errors.

---

* See paragraph 35 and paragraph 147.

145. Yet another view among German speaking teachers is represented by an *Austrian* writer who stresses the importance of an oral approach and opposes the use of signs but recommends finger spelling as an aid to the development of speech and lipreading[9].

146. All the *Scandinavian countries* subscribe to the aim of developing proficiency in oral communication and for this purpose use methods which are predominantly oral and fully exploit residual hearing. Nevertheless, in *Denmark* schools continue to use, for younger children, the combined method which is known as the mouth-hand system. This was developed by G. Forchhammer at the turn of the present century and is described in detail in a thesis accepted by the University of Copenhagen for the degree of Doctor of Philosophy and later published[10]. We have already indicated in paragraph 35 the phonemic nature of the mouth-hand system. The series of positions of the hand which accompany the spoken word were intended to be an outward indication of the inner positions of the organs of speech. Readers interested in contemporary comment on Dr. Forchhammer's work, including the developmental work, are referred to American Annals of the Deaf, 1899, 1901, and 1902, and The Teacher of the Deaf, 1917[11]. The last mentioned commentary, by W. Carey Roe, was on a series of articles by Dr. Forchhammer published in previous issues of The Teacher of the Deaf, 1916[11]. A handbook on the system by Tove Nielsen, Senior Teacher in the State School for the Deaf in Fredericia, was published in 1958[12]. This contains suggestions and instructions for teachers and simplifies earlier instructions, particularly in dispensing with a phonetic orthography used in some former manuals. The exercise material is given in traditional Danish orthography but consonants which are omitted or altered in speech are printed in italics.

147. The situation in the *United States of America* differs from that in most European countries in that there are two distinct and long established traditions. On the one hand there are schools and classes using purely oral methods; on the other there are those schools which operate what is known as the combined system, a term which refers not to a medium of communication but to a method of organising oral and manual teaching within the same school. For a concise historical summary of the development of the two main streams we cannot do better than quote from a paper which Dr. Powrie Vaux Doctor, editor of American Annals of the Deaf, kindly prepared for us.

'The first permanent school for the deaf in the United States was established at the American School for the Deaf in 1817 in Hartford, Connecticut, by Thomas Hopkins Gallaudet, who studied methods of teaching the deaf at the school for the deaf in Paris which had been founded by the Abbé de l'Epeé. On returning to the United States with Laurent Clerc, a deaf teacher of the deaf, he introduced into the United States manual communication which consisted of the language of signs and finger spelling. However, it must not be assumed that Gallaudet was not made aware of the oral method of teaching the deaf while in France. The first teacher of speech and speechreading in the United States was employed at the American School in 1836. At that time speech was termed articulation.

The first pure oral schools for the deaf in the United States were founded at The Clarke School for the Deaf in Northampton, Massachusetts, in 1867, and at The Lexington School for the Deaf in New York City the same year. The following year the organization now called The Conference of Executives of American Schools for the Deaf was founded at Gallaudet College. The previous year Edward Miner Gallaudet, the son of Thomas Hopkins Gallaudet, had visited the schools for the deaf in Europe. Although Edward Miner Gallaudet was impressed with the work done in speech and speechreading in Europe he still believed that many of the deaf, especially those born deaf, should be taught by manual communication. At the first meeting of The Conference of Executives of American Schools for the Deaf at Gallaudet College in 1868, the Combined System for teaching the deaf was adopted. This system provided for oral classes and manual classes in the same school. In general in most residential schools for the deaf in the United States the pupils in the pre-school and primary departments today are taught orally and are divided into oral and manual classes at the beginning of the Intermediate Department. Some schools in the United States, especially the New Mexico School for the Deaf, are using finger spelling in the beginning classes*. The Rochester School for the Deaf, which pioneered in teaching by finger spelling and speech† uses only the oral method in the primary department.‡

In the last decade in the United States, especially at Gallaudet College, the Simultaneous Method§ is coming into use'.

148. Further references to the education of deaf children in the United States of America are in the final section of this chapter dealing with research and experiment.

149. We have little information about established practice elsewhere which is of direct relevance to our terms of reference. Our attention was drawn however to an article by Mr. B. E. Reynolds in the *Australian* Teacher of the Deaf which provides a further example of the current use (at the Victorian School for the Deaf) of a combined method. Elsewhere in Australian schools, methods are predominantly oral. The article adds the interesting information that parents of pupils are expected to learn to communicate manually with their children[13]. In a joint communication from Mr. Reynolds and the present headmaster of the Victorian School we were informed: 'This school .... provides education for children whose deafness ranges from moderately severe to profound. The combined or simultaneous method is employed to communicate with and instruct all of the children. Speech is used at all times by the teacher, together with finger spelling and signs, supplemented where necessary by the written form and any other necessary media. Responses from the children are in speech, supplemented where necessary by finger spelling, gesture and the written form.' We understand that the signing used in teaching is based on that described in a book written in collaboration by members of the Dominican Order of nuns at Waratah School and the Christian Brothers at Castle Hill School, both in New South Wales[14].

---

* See paragraph 151(c) and footnotes.

† See paragraph 34.

‡ A member of H.M. Inspectorate who recently visited the U.S.A. has informed us that purely oral methods are not now used in the later years of the primary stage.

§ See paragraph 36.

Research and Experiment

150. We were not able to identify many research studies or experimental works bearing directly on the subject of our enquiry. We have already described (in paragraphs 128 to 137) the work which began experimentally in the *U.S.S.R.* in the early 1950's and led to a change of practice in all schools for deaf children. Elsewhere the major developments which concern us are the controlled experiments which are being carried out in the *United States of America* under the direction of Professor Stephen Quigley, Professor of Special Education in the Institute for Research on Exceptional Children, the University of Illinois. In describing his work to us Professor Quigley pointed out that controversy had continued for more than 100 years in the United States concerning the relative merits of the different communication methods used in instructing deaf students. In spite of the controversy, very few attempts had been made to study the problem systematically and objectively. These observations on a lack of objective studies apply with equal, or even greater force, in the United Kingdom.

151. The programme of research under Professor Quigley's direction consists of three studies as follows:

(a) a case study involving the exposure at home of deaf children aged two or younger to constant finger spelling and speech through their parents, a procedure to be continued over a period of years into the school years. (This study had not begun at the time of our meeting with Professor Quigley.)

(b) an experimental study comparing the effects of finger spelling on school children ranging from ages three and a half to five years. This study began at the Indiana School for the Deaf in 1964 and comparisons will be made with children in other residential schools using oral methods, including, it is hoped, a school where oral methods are applied as ideally as possible. Assessment of language and communication development was planned to begin in 1967.

(c) a survey study comparing the development of children in a number of schools where a combination of finger spelling and speech is used with comparable children in schools where finger spelling and speech are not systematically used throughout the schools. Nine residential schools are involved in three groups of three, each group consisting of an experimental school and two 'comparison' schools*. In two of the experimental schools finger spelling is not used in teaching until the post-primary stage. In the third experimental school, the New Mexico School for the Deaf in Santa Fe, finger spelling begins when children enter the school, usually about the age of five or six†*. The comparison schools all use oral methods in the early grades but provide manual classes for many of the older children. This study was the first to begin and some statistical analysis of the data collected had begun in 1966; but this is a large survey on which work is still in progress.

---

* We have since been informed by a member of H.M. Inspectorate, following his recent visit to the U.S.A., that the number of schools involved has been reduced to six, in three groups of two each; and that the New Mexico School now uses finger spelling with children starting school at the age of three.

† The combined use of finger spelling and speech in teaching young deaf children at the New Mexico School began in 1958. Marshall S. Hester, Litt.D., superintendent of the school, delivered a paper on this subject to the International Congress on the Education of the Deaf, held at Washington, D.C. in June, 1963. A copy is available at the R.N.I.D. Library, London[15].

152. The purpose of the studies is to determine what effects, if any, the use of finger spelling in combination with oral methods of instruction might have on the language, communication, and educational development of deaf children; and to determine if the age at which finger spelling is introduced is a critical factor. The decision to undertake this programme of research was influenced very largely by reports of results which were claimed for the experimental use of finger spelling with young deaf children in the U.S.S.R. While knowledge of the Russian research was limited, the extent of the claimed vocabulary development was considered to warrant investigation of the method in the United States. The findings of the American research programme will, of course, be of the greatest interest in this country.

153. Another recent study in the United States of relevance to our enquiry was that carried out by Dr. Jack Birch and Dr. E. Ross Stuckless on the relationship between early manual communication and later achievement of deaf children[16]. Thirty-eight deaf children whose parents had communicated with them by manual media during their infancy were matched with thirty-eight deaf children with whom manual media had not been used in infancy. The criterion of manual communication was the use of 100 or more discrete signs, which could include the symbols of the manual alphabet.

154. The conclusions reached are summarised in the research report as follows:
'1. Early manual communication appears to have no influence on the intelligibility of the deaf students' speech. This conclusion is drawn cautiously due to the unsatisfactory methods of testing for differences in the speech intelligibility of deaf children with and without early manual communication.
2. Early manual communication facilitates the acquisition of language in deaf students as manifest through comprehension in reading.
3. Early manual communication facilitates the acquisition of speech reading skills in deaf students.
4. Early manual communication facilitates the acquisition of language in deaf students as manifest through written expression.
5. Early manual communication has no negative influence on the psychosocial development of deaf children and probably has the effect of producing a level of psychosocial adjustment superior to that of the deaf child without such a communication system.
    Where differences exist in the basic language and language-mediating skills of deaf children with and without an early manual communication system, such differences favour the deaf child with the early manual communication.'

155. In studying this work we have noted that the investigators deliberately elimated from their sample children with central nervous disorders and that they also excluded children of deaf parents who had refrained from using signs. No steps were taken however to eliminate children brought up in an oral environment whose parents had not received skilled guidance during the children's infancy. The comparison therefore was between deaf children reared in a manual environment, from which stress through inability to communicate might be absent, and deaf children brought up orally by parents who might or might not have received skilled guidance. Although this is an important work, it is one which we feel could be repeated with advantage in a project designed to control

this additional variable factor. We also note that there was no analysis of the results as between pupils of the combined and oral schools. The work has been criticised elsewhere on the grounds that although statistically significant differences were found between the two groups the differences were small in absolute terms[17].

156. We refer finally to two pieces of work in *Scotland*. The first is a pilot study in progress in the Glasgow School for the Deaf where the new Paget systematic sign language has been used experimentally since January 1967 in the senior department of the school with a small group of children whose progress is being compared with that of a similar group taught by purely oral methods. Neither group contains children with disabilities additional to deafness. The organisation of teaching on a subject basis introduces complications in the sense that children in the Paget group are partly taught by teachers using oral methods only. Since this pilot scheme is of such recent origin and the groups of children are very small, no conclusions can be drawn but some interesting possibilities appear to be emerging in initial gains made by the experimental group. The school is also experimenting in the use of the new Paget system in teaching deaf children with additional handicaps.*

157. Information about a research study carried out in Scotland was sent to us by Mr. G. W. G. Montgomery, research psychologist at Donaldson's School for the Deaf. A paper by Mr. Montgomery was subsequently published in 'Annals'.[18] This was a study of 55 deaf school leavers to whom tests of speech, lipreading and intelligence were given and who were independently rated for speech, lipreading and manual communication by their teachers. In the summary it is stated that the interrelationships of tests and ratings were examined in order to discover whether the alleged incompatibility between oral skills and manual communication is observable statistically. No negative correlation was found. We note however that although pupils' comprehension of oral communication was investigated by lipreading tests there were no tests of their ability in the use of spoken language; the tests of speech were of articulation. His results therefore do not offer us evidence of the relationship between manual and oral *communication*.

REFERENCES

1. (a) A. G. Gerankina   The dactyl form of speech and its mastery. *Voprosy Defektologii.* Moscow: Lenin Pedagogical Institute, 1964, pp.175–97.

   (b) P. G. Guslistyi   The initial stages in teaching reading skills to dea mute children. *Doklady Akademii Pedagogicheskikh Nauk.* RSFSR Moscow: 1960, 4. (translated in 'Soviet Education' Vol. IV, No. 1, November 1961, pp.35–38, International Arts and Sciences Press, New York).

   (c) B. D. Korsunskaya   On methods of forming the independent speech of deaf and dumb children of pre-school age. *Proceedings of the Second Scientific Session on Defectology.* Moscow: APN, 1959, pp.38–47.

* We understand that experiments in the use of the new Paget system are also being made in the deaf/blind unit at Condover Hall School, Shrewsbury, maintained by the Royal National Institute for the Blind.

(d) B. D. Korsunskaya   *Teaching Speech to Deaf Pre-School Children.* Moscow: APN, 1960, p.170.

(e) B. D. Korsunskaya   Methodical instructions for the use of dactylic speech in teaching pre-school deaf children. *Spetsial'naya Shkola*, 1960, 97, 5–11.

(f) E. P. Kuz'micheva   Teaching deaf children whose speech is formed on a dactylogical basis to read and write. *Materials from a Scientific Conference on Defectology.* Moscow: APN, 1962, pp.81–6.

(g) E. N. Martsinovskaya   Correlation of oral and dactyl forms of speech of pupils in the school for the deaf. *Proceedings of the Third Scientific Session on Defectology.* Moscow: APN, 1960, pp.26–7.

(h) E. N. Martsinovskaya   The influence of finger spelling on the reproduction of the sound-syllabic structure of a word by deaf children. *Spetsial'naya Shkola*, 1961, 102, 22–8.

(i) N. A. Moreva   The teaching of the finger alphabet. *Proceedings of the Third Scientific Session on Defectology.* Moscow: APN, 1960, pp. 53–54.

(j) B. V. Morkovin   Experiment in teaching deaf pre-school children in the Soviet Union. *Volta Review*, 1960, 62, 260–3 and 266–8.

(k) B. V. Morkovin   Helping the deaf child toward adequate language and speech. Journal of Rehabilitation, May–June, 1963, Vol. XXIX, No. 3.

(l) N. G. Morozova   The development of the theory of pre-school education of the deaf. *Proceedings of the Second Scientific Session on Defectology.* Moscow: APN, 1959, pp.12–27.

(m) N. G. Morozova   Pre-school education of deaf children in the U.S.S.R. In *The Modern Educational Treatment of Deafness*, ed. by A. Ewing. Manchester University Press, 1960.

(n) N. G. Morozova and B. D. Korsunskaya   Teaching children of pre-school age. *SCR Soviet Educational Bulletin*, 1960, 7, 8–12.

(o) F. Srom   Sprachunterricht und Daktylogie. *Die Sonderschule*, 1965, 2, 84–8.

(p) M. F. Titova   Mastering the pronunciation of speech sounds by deaf mutes, beginning with the finger alphabet. *Spetsial'naya Shkola*, 1960, 95, 24–33.

(q) M. F. Titova   Pecularities in mastering pronunciation amongst deaf children who are beginning to learn speech through dactylic language. *Spetsial'naya Shkola*, 1960, 97, 20–8.

(r) M. F. Titova   On the correlation between the structure of a word in its spoken and written form. *Spetsial'naya Shkola*, 1960, 98, 23–7.

(s) M. F. Titova   The first steps in the dactyl acquisition of meaning in deaf children. *Doklady Akademii Pedagogicheskikh Nauk.* RSFSR Moscow: 1960, 3, 125–8.

(t) M. F. Titova   *Mastery by Deaf School Children of Word Pronunciation with Use of Dactylic Form of Speech.* Moscow: APN, 1963, p.100.

(u) G. L. Vygodskaya and
   B. D. Korsunskaya (Eds.)

The Formation of Speech in Young Pre-School Deaf Children. Moscow: Enlightenment Press, 1964, p.88.

(v) S. A. Zykov

Textbook for Deaf Children. Moscow: Uchpedgiz, Ministry of Education, 1962.

2. N. A. Moreva

Peculiarities of mastering speech by deaf pre-school children from two to five years. *Proceedings of the First International Conference of the Association for Special Education,* 1966, Association for Special Education Ltd., 39 Little Common, Stanmore, Middlesex, pp.315–316.

3. M. Greulich

Language teaching in the first two school years of the Soviet deaf and dumb school. *Neue Blätter fur Taubstummenbildung,* Heidelberg, 1965, pp.37–44.

4. H. G. Williams

The pre-school education of deaf children in Russia. *The Teacher of the Deaf,* 1960, LVIII 347, pp.330–344.

5. A. Grisoni-Colli

The child who does not talk. *Clinics in Developmental Medicine,* 13, p.96, Heinemann, 1964.

6. R. Arpaia

Dattilogia e commenta mimico. *Effeta,* 56, 1963, pp.181–188.

7. A. Ewing and
   A. Van Uden

The Education of the Deaf in the U.S.A. and the 'Combined Method'. *The Teacher of the Deaf,* LVIII, 344, pp.103–111.

8. E. Hebeler

Gebardensprache—anders gesehen (A different view on the sign language). *Neue Blätter fur Taubstummenbildung,* 18, 1964, 236–244, 321–331.

9. F. Höfler

Gedanken uber Gebarde und Handalphabet. *Neue Bl. Taubst.,* 18, 1964, 297–301.

10. G. Forchhammer

Om Nodvendigheden af Sikra Meddelelesmidler: Dovstumme under Ervisningen. (The need of a sure means of communication in the instruction of the deaf) Copenhagen: J. Frimodts, Fortag, 1903, p.300. Text available at R.N.I.D. Library, London, with Appendix 3 illustrating manual positions to be employed.

11. G. Forchhammer
    (contemporary reviews of his work)

American Annals of the Deaf, 1899, 44, 456–458; 1901, 46, 116–122, 1902, 47, 363–370. *The Teacher of the Deaf,* 1917, 89, 124–127, commenting on *a series of articles by Dr. Forchhammer* in *The Teacher of the Deaf,* 1916, 84, 185–192; 1917, 85, 4–10; and 1917, 86, 37–47.

12. T. Nielsen

Mund-Handsystemet, Vejledning for begyndere. Fredericia, Centraltrykkeriet—Johs Madsen, 1958,

13. B. E. Reynolds

Manualism—The Child, the Parent and the Teacher. *Australian Teacher of the Deaf,* 1, 1963, 14–15.

14. The teaching staffs of Waratah and Castle Hill Schools, New South Wales.

How to converse with the deaf in sign language. Davies-Carrington Printing Ltd., King Street, Newcastle, New South Wales, 1943.

15. M. S. Hester

Manual Communication. *Proceedings of the International Congress on the Education of the Deaf and of the 41st Meeting of American Instructors of the Deaf, Gallaudet College,* 1963, pp.211–221.

16. J. W. Birch & E. R. Stuckless

The relationship between early manual communication and later achievement of the deaf. University of Pittsburgh, May, 1964, p.58.

17. L. M. Dicarlo

Much ado about the obvious. *Volta Review*, April 1966, 68, 4, pp.269–273.

18. G. W. G. Montgomery

The relationship of oral skills to manual communication in profoundly deaf adolescents. *Annals*, September, 1966, pp.557–565.

Chapter VIII. Range and Nature of Evidence Obtained by the Committee

158. We now approach that part of our Report which will set out in summary the views put before us by witnesses. This chapter provides a preface indicating not only the range but also the nature of the evidence which we were able to obtain.

159. Invitations to submit evidence published in the press evoked a response from a number of interested persons, including many deaf people and friends or relatives of the deaf. In addition, we sent invitations to selected individuals and associations concerned with:

The professional education of teachers of the deaf;

the inspection of schools for the deaf;

the education and welfare of deaf children and adolescents, including those concerned as parents;

the welfare of deaf adolescents and adults;

medical aspects of deafness; and

the employment of the deaf.

Although deaf adults were among those submitting evidence in response to our general invitation we made special arrangements to supplement this and the evidence collected by associations representing the interests of deaf people. These arrangements are described in paragraphs 165 to 168.

160. It was our aim in selecting individuals to cover a wide sample of opinion and in all but a few cases those we approached felt able to submit memoranda.

161. We recognised that some associations whose views we sought would be unable to present evidence which represented the unanimous opinion of their entire membership and that they would find it impracticable to canvass the views of every member. We have noted that in all these cases the memorandum of evidence was prepared by members with relevant experience deputed by the association to undertake this task or by a standing committee acting on behalf of the association. We have accepted the evidence on that basis, recognising that it was the aim of ad hoc or standing committees to reflect majority opinion within the association. However, one association, the National Council of Missioners and Welfare Officers to the Deaf, conducted enquiries among its members which enabled it to present the general principles outlined in its evidence as being held unanimously by the entire membership. We understand that the great majority of workers among the deaf adults of Great Britain are members of the National Council.

162. The British Deaf and Dumb Association also canvassed the views of its members, inviting those who felt strongly either way about the subject of our enquiry to submit comments. To assist members who might have difficulty in framing their views, the Association devised a simple form, which it asked members to sign if the wording reflected their views and experience. The form read as follows:

'I am deaf. I know because of my deafness that finger spelling and sign language should be used in schools and it is very important in my life.'

We appreciate the motives of the Association in wishing to help its members in making their views known and we have noted that a very large number of deaf members signed this form. But we are bound to point out that the method by which their views were obtained allowed for the introduction of an unknown degree of bias. In saying this we have no grounds for suggesting that a different method would have produced a different result; we wish simply to record the uncertain validity of the evidence.

163. It can, of course, be argued that opinion, irrespective of its colour or source, is irrelevant unless based upon objective findings from controlled studies since only in this way can fully valid evidence be obtained. But carefully weighed opinion based upon experience and trained observation has its own value and can also give many helpful indications of the directions in which research may be required. Much of the evidence we received was of this kind and, indeed, could not have been otherwise if, as we understand, there has been little systematic use of finger spelling or signing in schools for the deaf in this country for over 30 years and most research workers have been interested in other aspects of the education of the deaf.

164. We received thoughtful and closely argued memoranda, both from those whose experience had led them to conclude that there was a place for finger spelling or signing, or both, in teaching deaf pupils and also from those who took the opposite view. We also received much assistance from those witnesses who appeared before us in person and who had, almost without exception, previously submitted written evidence. Understandably, however, since the subject of our enquiry is one which, in the past, has aroused passionate controversy, some of the papers sent to us threw more light on the prejudices of the writer than on the problems under discussion. This was true of adherents of both the main points of view, but it seems to us that one particularly regrettable aspect of the controversy is the belief which appeared to have grown in the minds of some of those who wrote to us that teachers of the deaf, out of perversity, have entered into a tacit conspiracy to frustrate experiment with any methods of teaching deaf pupils which are not purely oral. We would emphasise that this view was not expressed or implied in the evidence of any of the associations and we hope that it is a view which will not survive the conclusion of our enquiry.

165. The special arrangements which we made to obtain evidence from deaf adults were designed, so far as possible, to obtain factual information about methods of communication in use in various circumstances, although other factual information was also obtained and opportunity was provided for comment. We obtained evidence in two ways. We ourselves invited a small number of deaf adults to appear before us in person; they included witnesses who relied upon the help of an interpreter as well as witnesses who communicated fluently by oral means. In addition, with the kind assistance of the Ministry of Health and the Inner London Education Authority, we arranged for about 50 young deaf people to be interviewed in their homes or at social clubs.

166. Although we could undoubtedly have approached a far greater number of witnesses by postal questionnaire we decided not to adopt this course. Many deaf people experience severe linguistic difficulties and are dependent upon people with normal hearing for explanation or interpretation. The greatest care is needed to establish whether and to what extent the views they express are entirely their own and have not been modified or unconsciously influenced by

their transmission through an intermediary. It would have been impossible to determine what help had been received in the preparation of answers to a postal questionnaire.

167. To avoid variations arising from different approaches to interpretation, we sought the help of only one interviewer to visit the young people who agreed to take part in the survey. Miss Brooke-Hughes of the Ministry of Health, who undertook the work of interviewing and to whom we are greatly indebted, was very conscious of the problems associated with an enquiry of this kind and we are confident that due to the care she took to avoid an approach which might have influenced answers she overcame the difficulties as far as it was possible for any interviewer to do.

168. This was a limited survey, although it was very time-consuming in both the preparatory work, to make clearly understood arrangements for interviews, and the interviews themselves. Because of its limited scope it cannot be assumed that exactly similar results would be obtained from larger surveys. Its main findings, with a summary of other evidence from deaf witnesses, are reported in paragraphs 259 to 261.

169. Some welfare workers who submitted evidence based this on surveys which they had initiated themselves. One such survey was carried out by the senior welfare officer employed by a county health authority in the south of England, who arranged for questionnaires to be completed by some 200 registered deaf persons resident or formerly resident in the county, or resident elsewhere, but attending clubs for the deaf in the county. This was a simple enquiry designed to elicit facts about methods of communication used and preferred by the deaf persons, but on analysis we found that it did not add to the evidence presented to us by the National Council of Missioners and Welfare Officers to the Deaf.

170. We did not seek direct evidence of the defective speech of deaf children. This is a well-known characteristic of the handicap and it is within our personal knowledge that their speech is often unintelligible and frequently defective. Evidence of this was provided in the report of the survey to which we referred in paragraph 18.

Chapter IX. The Advantages Claimed for Education by Oral Methods

171. In this chapter we shall describe the opinions which were offered in support of exclusively oral methods of teaching and identify the children in respect of whom these views were held and the types of experience on which they were based.

Partially hearing pupils

172. We begin by referring to the area of discussion where our witnesses were, for the most part, in general agreement about the desirability of using oral methods and no others. This was the case in relation to the education of partially hearing pupils. We did not invite written evidence specifically relating to these pupils, but discussion of their education arose naturally in oral evidence and views were also volunteered in some of the memoranda we received. We, ourselves, as we have already stated, considered the education of the deaf in the context of educational arrangements made for all children with impaired hearing.

173. It was not always possible to be sure of the basis on which written evidence distinguished between deaf and partially hearing pupils, but after studying the evidence in the light of the definitions and criteria in paragraphs 1 and 2 we are reasonably confident that the majority of witnesses expressing a view believed that partially hearing pupils, properly so described, should be educated by exclusively oral methods.

Deaf pupils

174. *Perhaps the most remarkable feature of the evidence was the fact that no organisation or individual witness whom we approached suggested that oral methods and no other methods were entirely appropriate for all deaf pupils at all stages of their education.* This is an important fact worth underlining, since the view is still held that there is a school of thought in this country which would exclude in all circumstances the use of any methods not covered by the definition of oral methods in Chapter III. Having said this, we must make it clear that a number of witnesses nonetheless considered that oral methods were the most appropriate for the majority of deaf pupils throughout school life, not only because these children have to grow up and take their place in a world in which oral communication prevails, but also because oral methods are, in their view, the most effective instrument for the teaching of language, the development of thinking, the acquisition of knowledge and the development of personality. Essentially, their disagreement with other witnesses was about means rather than ends since there was a widely shared belief, as we pointed out in Chapter II, that deaf children should be brought up to take their place, so far as possible, in hearing society, and most witnesses, with this in view, regarded oral proficiency as a desirable aim.

175. Advocates of the use of oral methods for the majority of deaf children are sometimes referred to as pure oralists. In so far as our evidence was representative of opinion in this country, it suggests that the general use of this term is no longer justified because it implies a rejection of the use of natural gesture. It is safe to say that within the schools a good many 'pure oralists' today would not exclude gesture of the kind and amount used naturally by people with normal

hearing in the society in which the deaf child grows up. (There was, however, a little evidence of the discouragement or prohibition of natural gesture in the results of our enquiries about present practices of schools in methods of communication (Chapter VI and Appendix B.)

176. Some witnesses who advocated the use of oral methods and no others for the majority of deaf children pointed out that it could not be assumed that children educated by these methods who were failing to make progress would necessarily do better if they were introduced to manual media of communication; there might be some other cause of their lack of progress. This point was made in a memorandum published by the National College of Teachers of the Deaf which was brought to our attention by the Executive Committee of the College: 'It is over-simplification to suggest, as is sometimes done, that the use of manual or combined methods would automatically produce higher standards of literacy. When children fail to progress linguistically under the oral method, a careful analysis should be made of the reason for their difficulties.'[1] The same point was stressed by a number of individual witnesses, including Emeritus Professor Sir Alexander Ewing.

177. Some of these witnesses were also convinced that oral methods, meaning the whole range of techniques described in Chapter III, had not yet had a fair trial everywhere. Pre-school training and arrangements for giving guidance to parents were not of a uniformly high standard and teachers in some schools had to contend with over-size classes. These witnesses claimed that where there were good services for children with impaired hearing, both inside and outside school, oral methods were proving their worth and that, in fact, it was becoming increasingly possible to educate children with very severe hearing losses from birth or early infancy as partially hearing pupils although formerly they would have been treated as deaf. Claims of this nature were made not only by teachers of the deaf but also by those of our witnesses who had undertaken or directed applied research or whose views were based on clinical experience.

The education of younger children

178. Some of the arguments advanced in support of oral methods were related to a particular stage of education. The needs of children at the primary stage were specially emphasised in the written evidence of the Executive Committee of the National College of Teachers of the Deaf. In view of the weight of teaching opinion represented by this evidence we quote in full the paragraphs dealing with the question whether finger spelling should be used in the primary education of deaf children without additional disabilities.*

'In the early stages the development of language and oral communication are complex and mutually inter-dependent processes. They depend upon specific training of the visual and aural senses before precise measurements of sight and hearing are possible, and long before mental development is sufficient to allow the introduction of spelling either in the durable printed form or in the transient pattern of finger spelling. Although experimental work is being carried out on

---

* In the case of some mentally handicapped children with a profound or severe hearing loss, the National College suggested that their only means of communication might prove to be a simple system of signs. The College made no proposal that finger spelling should be used in teaching deaf children with additional disabilities.

the use of finger spelling in nursery and infant classes in the U.S.A., post-war evidence in this country has clearly demonstrated the great benefits resulting from early auditory training and the optimum use of modern hearing aids. The majority opinion of the N.C.T.D. is that finger spelling is not suitable for use with pre-school, nursery or infant school deaf children.

The ability to read and write begins to develop at the infant/junior stage and the growth of language, lipreading and speech skills becomes more rapid. The potential value of finger spelling as an aid to lipreading must be assessed in relation to the value of the printed form of spelling in normal teaching situations, i.e. with small classes in rooms specially equipped with electronic aids, blackboards, writing materials, etc. The greater speed of finger spelling must be considered together with the transience of its pattern: the abilities of children to comprehend the meanings of successions of letters compared with their abilities to comprehend printed syllables or whole words must be carefully assessed: the long term effects of establishing a habit of reliance upon a relatively little used mode of communication cannot be overlooked. Difficulties experienced in the teaching of reading to normal children have led to numerous experiments, and if full advantage is to be taken of such modern developments, the traditional classroom methods would appear to be preferable. The N.C.T.D. Executive Committee is of the opinion that finger spelling is not suitable for general use in infant/junior schools.'

The education of older children
179. The Executive Committee went on to point out that there is a wider range of opinions among teachers of the deaf about media of communication in secondary education. Even so, it appeared to the Executive Committee that the majority of teachers of the deaf held the view that finger spelling is neither necessary nor desirable in the two selective secondary schools.*

Slow learning children
180. The belief that oral methods are both desirable and practicable for the majority of deaf pupils was strongly held by those members of the teaching staffs of the two University Departments in England responsible for training teachers of the deaf† who responded to our invitation to submit evidence individually. This evidence touched on the specific problems of slow learning children in the light of the suggestion sometimes made that these children would be helped by finger spelling. It reached the conclusion that this method of communication presented greater difficulties than those of speech and lipreading for a backward child since it involved the complications of learning to spell and retaining that knowledge and of symbolising from an alphabet. These witnesses did not suggest, however, that oral methods should be persisted with to the exclusion of all other methods throughout the school life of backward deaf pupils. (c.f. paragraph 178 above and footnote).

181. It was the view of Emeritus Professor Sir Alexander Ewing, when giving oral evidence, that only in exceptional cases would it be appropriate to consider

---

* The Mary Hare Grammar School, Newbury, Berkshire, and Burwood Park School, Oxted, Surrey.

† The University of Manchester Department of Audiology and Education of the Deaf and the University of London Institute of Education.

introducing non-oral methods. Sir Alexander Ewing gave us helpful information from the results of his own clinical work and from research studies carried out under his direction at the University of Manchester about factors affecting the progress of deaf children educated by oral methods. Summarising his conclusions based on these observations, he said that he would regard combined methods as a last resort for children failing to achieve any score in language after all that was possible had been done to help them. In the extreme circumstances which might justify a decision to introduce manual media as a supplementary aid to learning, it might be desirable to take the decision while the child was still quite young, provided that his learning difficulties had been thoroughly investigated in the light of his medical history and that the manual media chosen were appropriate to these difficulties.

Children of average or above-average ability

182. In addition to the problems of children who are slow to learn, evidence dealt with the question whether education by completely oral methods enabled deaf pupils of average or above-average ability to realise their full potential. We have already referred to the view of the Executive Committee of the National College of Teachers of the Deaf that the majority of its members consider that finger spelling is neither necessary nor desirable in the two selective secondary schools. This view was reflected in the remarks of some of our individual witnesses. The head teacher of one secondary school for the deaf thought that although the use of finger spelling by deaf children of high ability might improve accuracy of communication and, possibly, attainment as measured by examination results, these gains had to be considered in the light of the long term aim of enabling deaf children to take their place in the hearing world. If children learned to rely on finger spelling they would have fewer incentives and opportunities to practice the oral skills, without which they could not mix freely with hearing people. This head teacher thought that the long term view should prevail even in the case of children whose potential ability to integrate might be in doubt. More generally however there were differences of opinion as to the value of finger spelling in the secondary education of children capable of reaching the middle or higher levels of attainment.

Methods in relation to aims

183. The desire not to cut deaf children off from the wider community was felt keenly by all those who most strongly advocated the exclusive use, wherever possible, of oral methods. These witnesses did not generally claim that deaf children were capable of integrating fully with the hearing world; some felt that the ability to receive oral communications through lipreading was a substantial justification for perseverance with oral methods even where capacity for oral expression was limited. But they did claim that it was important for deaf children to develop oral attitudes and above all to have the opportunity of normal linguistic development. Many of these witnesses thought that this would not be possible if manual media of communication were used, even if only in a supplementary role, either because their use would directly interfere with the development of correct, connected language or simply because it would limit the time available for practising the normal linguistic skills of speech, reading and writing.

REFERENCE

1. National College of Teachers of the Deaf, *Educational Provision for Children with Defective Hearing*, obtainable from the Hon. Circulation Secretary, National College of Teachers of the Deaf, Royal West of England School for the Deaf, Topsham Road, Exeter.

Chapter X. The Advantages Claimed for Education by Manual and Combined Media of Communication

The use of manual media of communication

184. None of our evidence led us to believe that there is an identifiable body of opinion in this country which would support the re-introduction of either finger spelling or signing or both to the exclusion of oral methods in the education of deaf children generally, although a few people who wrote individually in response to our published request for evidence seemed to hold this view. These writers were either deaf themselves or related to deaf people, but they did not appear to represent a widely held opinion among deaf adults. *All our evidence from associations representing deaf or hard of hearing people, and from individuals and organisations concerned professionally with deaf children or adults, emphasized to a greater or lesser degree that it is important that opportunities should be available for children to learn to communicate by speech, lipreading and, where possible, the use of residual hearing.* Where there was support for the general use of finger spelling or signing or both, these media were usually seen either as aids to the establishment of oral communication or as desirable supplements. Where it was thought that manual communication was needed in individual cases as a substitute for oral communication, the assumption was made that there would have been an attempt to educate by oral methods. The cases where it was suggested that attempts at oral communication might be largely abandoned where those where children failed to make measurable progress; or were slow learning as a result of additional disability, emotional disturbance or lack of appropriate special educational treatment at a sufficiently early stage; or were inaccessible through speech and language because of a disorder of communication unrelated to their deafness.

185. Among deaf children whose communication difficulties cause particular anxiety, it is perhaps the last mentioned group whose problems seem the most daunting. (See also paragraph 88.) Clinical studies suggest that children with speech and language disorders unrelated to deafness form a heterogeneous group and that further studies are required to establish the nature and quality of the responses to sound of which children with these disorders may be capable.[1] Further studies are also needed to establish the extent to which they may be capable of developing language. In the meantime, teachers in schools for the deaf are faced with the immediate, practical problem of creating a channel of communication with these children since, without this, not only can no educational progress be made but the risks of emotional disturbance and mental illness become very real. The basic need for communication in some form cannot be denied without disastrous consequences. It may be that until clearer indications can be given by medical science as to the nature and extent of the disabilities of children who appear to be inaccessible through speech and language, the use of gestures, mime and simple signs is not only unavoidable but desirable. There was little in our evidence to dispute this point of view.

The use of combined media of communication

186. We now turn to that part of our evidence which was concerned with modes of communication in which finger spelling or signing or both are combined in various ways with spoken language, either in accordance with a prescribed

63

system or to suit the needs of individual children as judged by their teachers. We propose to describe the types of combined media which were suggested as likely to be helpful and the purposes they are considered to serve. In the following chapter we shall indicate what views on these media and on the place of finger spelling and signing generally were held by various groups of witnesses.

187. It should perhaps be emphasized that those who advocate the combined use in schools of oral and manual media of communication attach at least as much importance to the teaching of reading and writing as do those who recommend the use of oral media alone. This is common ground. There are, however, differences of view and practice in the teaching profession as to the stage at which reading and writing should be introduced in the education of children with impaired hearing. Some teachers of the deaf believe that the concept of reading readiness can be paid too much service and that reading and writing should be started at a very early stage in order to provide an additional means of promoting language development.

Speech and finger spelling

(a) *For young children*

188. Evidence from witnesses and from our enquiry into current practice (Chapter VI and Appendix B) showed that finger spelling is used only to a very limited extent in this country in teaching young children; and, few witnesses suggested that methods comparable with those used in the U.S.S.R. or in Denmark should be introduced here. However, some witnesses thought that the possibility should be explored of using finger spelling more extensively and systematically at an early stage in view of the extreme difficulty of correcting distorted language patterns once these had become established. Reference was made to the possibility of using finger spelling at a very early stage so that children learn to recognise whole words even when they do not recognise single letters. As reported in paragraph 118, our attention was drawn to recently started experiments in a school for the deaf where nursery/infant children are being taught through a combination of lipreading and one-handed finger spelling.

(b) *For older children*

189. The combination of finger spelling with speech was also suggested for older children. Witnesses stated or implied that the extent to which oral methods should be supplemented would be largely a matter for the professional discretion of individual teachers. There would be two distinct although inter-related aims. The first would be to extend vocabulary and knowledge of language forms by supplementing the linguistic gains achieved through lipreading, residual hearing, reading and writing. A reciprocal benefit would occur in the improvement of lipreading resulting from an extended knowledge of language and vocabulary. The second aim would be to accelerate the pace of learning over the whole curriculum. Improvement would be possible not only in the rate at which children absorbed information but also in the speed of their responses in class. With reasonable fluency in finger spelling they could express themselves in the give and take of a lesson with greater ease than if they were expected to rely solely on the articulation of speech.

(c) *For children found to have difficulties in lipreading*

190. Some people maintain that lipreading is intrinsically so difficult that finger spelling should be used in teaching all deaf children. Others suggest that it is necessary only for those who experience severe difficulties in lipreading. No attempt was made by witnesses to prescribe precise techniques for use with children having these special difficulties but it seems reasonable to suppose that, in recommending the use of finger spelling to supplement residual hearing in these circumstances, they had in mind that teachers would finger spell, if not continuously, then at least more extensively than to children with better lipreading ability. (Certain limitations of finger spelling in overcoming the phonemic difficulties of lipreading were pointed out in the footnote to paragraph 70). The extent to which finger spelling was considered a suitable additional medium of communication in these circumstances depended upon the cause of the lipreading difficulty and other associated factors. For example, a deaf child with poor sight but with no other handicap was thought likely to be helped, whereas a child with a specific speech and language disorder, or unable to lipread through inability to concentrate, was expected to be equally handicapped in reading finger spelling.

(d) *For school leavers*

191. Several witnesses suggested that all deaf pupils, before leaving school, should be taught to finger spell so that they might have a relaxed method of communication with other deaf people. This was not regarded as the learning of a combined method of communication; but, in practice, children brought up orally would probably continue to speak while finger spelling. Nor was the proposal primarily related to school purposes, although it could hardly be implemented without having some effect on the children's work in their last year at school.

Speech and finger spelling with a minimal use of signs

192. One witness proposed that speech and finger spelling, with lipreading and the use of residual hearing, should all be combined and that the finger spelling should be used simultaneously and continuously with the oral media. Some small use of signs might be helpful but was not essential. It was suggested that this method should be adopted from the outset in nursery departments for deaf children, supplemented as early as possible and increasingly by the use of the written word, and should be continued at least for the first half of school life. Its aim in using all channels of communication simultaneously would be to give children the best opportunities of rapid progress in the understanding and use of language without depriving them of the opportunity of learning to talk. Speaking from experience of nursery departments in schools for the deaf, the witness recommending this method said that it was possible for a child to spend two or three years receiving training in speech, lipreading and auditory discrimination and yet leave the nursery department with language amounting to no more than a vocabulary of a few words.

Speech and finger spelling supplemented by signs

193. There was a body of opinion which supported a greater use of signs in a combined medium while still regarding signs as being subsidiary to the other elements, including finger spelling. For this reason, other recommendations in

respect of this particular combination of media did not differ substantially from those described in paragraphs 189 and 190 above, either in the manner in which it was suggested that the combined media should be used or in the purposes which were thought to be served. Signs were seen mainly as a convenient means of providing intermittent relief from monotony in finger spelling or as a way of marking separations between words which might not be readily seen in an uninterrupted flow of finger spelling.

Speech and signing or gesturing

194. Relatively little evidence was offered on the use of speech with conventional signs as the sole manual supplement; but a number of witnesses emphasised the value of natural gesture, especially in teaching young children, for example, in telling them stories and as an aid to the development of language forms.

195. We note that the revised Paget systematic sign language (see paragraphs 32 (c), 73 and 74), where it is being used experimentally to teach deaf children, is usually accompanied by speech.

Speech and signing supplemented by finger spelling

196. Here it is necessary to distinguish between a situation in which manual media of communication may assume the major or possibly the only effective role (as in paragraph 184 and 185) and those situations envisaged by witnesses who see manual media as a helpful supplement in a predominantly oral system. The latter subsidiary role for signs and finger spelling had its advocates who saw this combined medium as a means of enlarging vocabulary and the range of meanings within vocabulary, and as a way of imparting greater quantities of information. They also pointed to its potency as an expressive medium, to the aesthetic satisfaction derived from skilful performance and to the opportunity for release from the constraints of communication confined to media which are unnatural to deaf people.

197. Among deaf adults, speech and signs offer reciprocal gains in clarity. For example, where only a generic sign is available, the lipread word (which may also be partly heard) can indicate the particular class of object. Conversely, a sign for a category may help to explain the meaning of an unfamiliar word for a particular object. (The signs used do not consist exclusively of conventional signs; natural gestures and mime also play a part.) These advantages, it was suggested, would be likely to result from the combined use of speech and signs in the teaching of deaf children. The role of finger spelling would be to make good deficiencies in the vocabulary of conventional signs, particularly when new and difficult technical terms have to be used, and to supply visually certain parts of speech not normally signed.

REFERENCE

1. I. G. Taylor, *Hearing in Relation to Language Disorders in Children*, British Journal of Disorders of Communication, Vol. 1, No. 1, 1966.

Chapter XI. The Views of Witnesses

198. In this chapter we survey the whole range of evidence by reference to its source.

Teachers of the deaf

199. *The corporate view of teachers of the deaf*, as expressed to us by the Executive Committee of the National College of Teachers of the Deaf, differed from the views of some of the individual teachers whose help we sought or who wrote to us in response to our published request for evidence. The aim of the National College was to express, so far as possible, the majority view of its members. Our purpose was to seek information from a group of teachers of long and varied experience who were, collectively, familiar with every aspect of the education of deaf children. At the same time we wanted to ensure, so far as possible, that every point of view relevant to our terms of reference was heard. We believe that by these two means we have gained an adequate knowledge of the range and strength of opinion among teachers and we shall set out the views both of the National College and of the group of individual teachers.

200. In paragraphs 178 and 179 we have indicated the corporate view of the membership of the National College on the place of finger spelling in the education of deaf children. We understand that this may be interpreted as applying to combined media generally and that the Executive Committee of the National College have reason to believe that a majority of members takes the view that these are entirely inappropriate for children of nursery and infant school age. The majority of the Executive Committee believes that combined media are equally undesirable at the junior stage for most children and at the senior stage for pupils of above average intelligence and ability. As previously stated, views range more widely in respect of other senior pupils but the College has emphasised that it should not be automatically assumed that manual media would succeed where oral media have failed (paragraph 176). Subject to this reservation, however, it is the stated policy of the College that if the use of signs and finger spelling seems likely to result in the general all-round development of a child who has not made progress linguistically under the oral method, then these additional media of communication should be introduced. In its statement of policy, a distinction is made between those deaf children the College describes as generally retarded in linguistic development and those with a good comprehension of written and spoken language but unintelligible speech. It has made no recommendation that manual media of communication should be used in the education of the latter. Finally, it is the view of the College that children who need the additional help of finger spelling or signs or both should not remain in schools with children taught by purely oral methods.

201. Most of the *individual teachers* whose views we sought were heads of special schools for children with impaired hearing. Between them and as individuals, these witnesses had experience of teaching pupils of all ages and of all degrees and types of intelligence and nearly all had some personal experience in the use of finger spelling or signs or both in school. Some were also widely informed about the problems and achievements of deaf adults.

202. There were of course many nuances and varying emphases in the evidence given by these witnesses. However, in broad terms there was support for two

67

main points of view. On the one hand, there were those whose opinions corresponded with the corporate view of the membership of the National College of Teachers of the Deaf. On the other, there were those who doubted the efficacy of teaching most deaf pupils by oral methods alone. The first group of witnesses argued that although theoretically it may be possible to achieve good standards of language through the supplementary use of finger spelling (and signs, if used appropriately), in practice the linguistic standards which are achieved are lower, or at the best no higher, than those achieved by purely oral methods. At the same time, proficiency in oral communication is reduced by the smaller effort put into the practice of this skill.

203. These teachers recognised that there is however a group of children, a minority in their view, who do not make adequate progress when taught by purely oral methods. These children should have the additional help of finger spelling or signs and should be transferred to separate schools or departments of schools so that they do not hold back the oral progress of other children by familiarising them with manual media of communication. Since several witnesses suggested that this minority consisted mainly, if not entirely, of children with additional handicaps, it is worth recording that it seemed to be a commonly held opinion that there is a growing number of additionally handicapped children in special schools for the deaf. Some statistical evidence was presented to us, relating to a group of boarding schools, which appeared to support this opinion; it is also supported by the evidence referred to in paragraph 5. No national figures are available, however, and we believe that the position may vary from one school to another, depending partly on admissions policies.

204. Adherents of the other main point of view considered that the majority of deaf pupils cannot make sufficient progress if they are taught by oral methods alone because of the linguistic deprivation from which they suffer from birth or early infancy and the extreme difficulties they experience both in lipreading and in interpreting amplified sound. These are intrinsically difficult processes made infinitely more so by a deaf child's lack of naturally acquired language. Writing of the teaching of language to deaf pupils, the National College of Teachers of the Deaf has said 'Unlike other forms of language teaching, there is neither a mother tongue from which to elaborate, nor a vernacular with which to explain.' Having regard to these difficulties, the second group of teachers believed that finger spelling or signs or both, in various modes of combination with oral media, would bring about a general improvement in linguistic and other attainments, although they acknowledged and regretted the lack of experimental evidence from controlled studies.

205. This group of witnesses was itself divided, although there was some overlapping of views. There were those who supported the early use of manual media, usually finger spelling but in some cases the judicious use of signs, as an aid to the establishment of oral communication and to lay the foundations of language (paragraphs 188 and 192); and there were others who envisaged that manual media would not usually be introduced until later, possibly not until the secondary stage, when the children's need to formulate and express new ideas and deal with new experiences becomes urgent and runs ahead of their ability to acquire new language through oral methods of education (paragraphs 189 and 193). All witnesses in this group, however, recognised the needs of slow learning children with additional handicaps for whom special methods might be necessary from an early stage.

Those concerned with the full-time professional education of teachers

206. In paragraphs 180 and 181 we have indicated the general view expressed to us by members of staffs of the University Departments responsible for training teachers of the deaf and by Emeritus Professor Sir Alexander Ewing, formerly head of the University of Manchester Department of Audiology and Education of the Deaf. These witnesses emphasised that there were a number of preconditions of progress by oral methods of education and that some of these seemed to be more important than others. Key factors in successful oral education appeared to include early detection and assessment of hearing impairment, the skilled guidance of parents and the auditory training of young children, consistently good oral teaching in school, and close and continuing co-operation between home and school. In support of the beneficial effects of good early training and guidance, Sir Alexander Ewing gave us details of a study of two small groups of junior deaf pupils who were included in a larger controlled study of the linguistic growth of various groups of pupils with impaired hearing. The subsidiary study was concerned with those pupils who were the ten highest and ten lowest scorers among the junior deaf pupils in the main investigation. Their results were studied in the light of additional information about the children which was available to the University. This established that the lowest scoring deaf children, whose hearing losses were comparable with those of the best scoring group, were children who had suffered a limitation in the amount or quality of early training. In two cases emotional disturbance may also have been a factor. The children with the best scores had nearly all received good home training and guidance under expert supervision. Intelligence tests were also administered and although there was some correlation with scores in the linguistic tests, two of the worst scorers in vocabulary achieved an above-average grade in the intelligence test. (Sir Alexander also quoted an example of very successful oral education begun early at school when home training was impracticable and did not at all wish to exclude the possibility of this.)

207. In the light of these and other investigations and observations made over many years, Sir Alexander Ewing had reached the conclusion, reported in paragraph 181, that the use of combined media should be regarded as a last resort for children failing to achieve any score in language after all that was possible had been done to help them. Furthermore, he believed, as did a number of other witnesses, that children who appeared to need manual media of communication as a supplementary aid to learning should be taught separately from children taught by oral methods and that the two groups of children should not mix out of school.

208. Although other members of the University staff concerned had arrived at broadly similar conclusions, there were particular aspects of evidence which should be mentioned as indicative of individual differences of approach or emphasis. They were as follows:

(i) Finger spelling might be used as a minor aid, an adjunct to make communication more speedy and reliable, in the teaching of intelligent deaf children with no central nervous damage. This would be acceptable only if the children had language which was firmly established and understood the written patterns.

(ii) Deaf pupils with additional handicaps, especially those involving impaired intellectual functioning, may well need the help of signs and gestures. It was held that finger spelling was an unsuitable medium for teaching slow learning children.

(iii) An empirical approach may also be justified with children working well below their potential at the secondary stage. This might include the use of finger spelling or possibly of signs or gestures.

(iv) Among children who make little or no progress by oral methods there are some who begin to acquire language by reading. It was thought that their progress might be accelerated by combining finger spelling with reading and writing.

Inspectors of special education

209. We invited evidence from H.M. Inspectors of Schools with special responsibilities for the inspection of educational arrangements for deaf and partially hearing pupils in the United Kingdom and from inspectors of special education serving, or formerly serving, with several of the larger local education authorities. Between them these witnesses, prior to their appointment as inspectors, had a variety of experience of work with deaf children both inside and outside special schools. As inspectors all had additional responsibilities outside the field of deaf education.

210. In broad terms their evidence had two differing emphases. On the one hand there was one witness who held that since not all deaf pupils can achieve their maximum potential if they are educated by oral methods alone, there was a clear case for the supplementation of these methods by finger spelling and signs. The pupils for whom this would be specially appropriate would be those of average or dull intelligence, of whom the dullest might find finger spelling too difficult. On the other hand, there was the more general view that although manual media of communication may be helpful either to supplement oral methods or where oral methods have failed, and had indeed been shewn to be helpful in instances known to the witnesses, there was an absence of evidence from research to substantiate this as a general truth. Moreover, both observation and experience suggested that the wide variety of degrees of success in helping deaf pupils to acquire a command of language may be largely due to factors other than the medium of communication used. Although critical of aspects of practice in oral methods of education, several of these witnesses, like other groups, warned against 'the fallacy of the ideal alternative'.

211. Nonetheless, all suggested ways in which manual media might be used empirically, particularly in the imparting of information and with the object of removing strain in communication, whether in teaching deaf children with no additional difficulties or, at the other extreme, in establishing contact with children for whom any form of communication is justified to avert emotional instability. Most saw the probable place of finger spelling as an aid to the speedier imparting of information and not as a means by which children can acquire a correct knowledge of language or fluency in its use. But a suggestion was made that for senior pupils whose basic knowledge of language was well developed finger spelling might be used to impart further knowledge of language as well as information on subject matter. One witness doubted the value of introducing finger spelling for the first time at the secondary stage to retarded pupils because of the difficulty experienced in adapting such pupils to new ways of learning.

212. In so far as inspectors saw a place for signs it was also mainly as a means of accelerating the acquisition of knowledge and possibly only as an adjunct to finger spelling in the teaching of older pupils with well developed language.

213. Most of the inspectors we consulted thought that research was required to establish whether or not the use of finger spelling or signs or both would bring about an improvement in the linguistic and other attainments of deaf children. It will nevertheless be clear that they did not suggest that the absence of evidence from research should inhibit present practice with pupils demonstrably failing to make adequate progress under purely oral methods of education. In addition to the multiply-handicapped, for whom witnesses in every category saw a need for the use of a wide variety of visual aids to education and of media of communication in addition to lipreading and reading, it was suggested that the critical group were those children who have very severe hearing losses approaching total loss of hearing. Within this group, experience suggested that unless most of the relevant factors listed in Chapter V were favourable, oral ability would nevitably be very limited. Since many of these factors related either to events in the very early life of a child or to his life situation generally, it was often possible, where adequate medical, educational and social records were available, to make an educational prognosis at a relatively early stage. Nonetheless, in view of the necessity for deaf children to grow up and take their place in a hearing society, the general feeling among inspectors was that purely oral methods of education should be persisted in at least through the primary school for all children except possibly those who are severely disturbed emotionally, or multiply-handicapped or have obscure neurological conditions. Their views on this were, of course, subject to findings from research on the possible place of finger spelling or signs in early education as an aid to the establishment of oral communication and the acquisition of language.

214. As to the separation of children taught through a combination of manual and oral media of communication, views varied according to the place allotted to the manual media. Where this was very limited, relating only to the use of manual media to accelerate the acquisition of knowledge by senior pupils with an adequately developed command of language, separation appeared to be unnecessary. Senior pupils able to make sufficient progress through oral media alone seemed unlikely to be harmed by finger spelling (or the use of signs as an adjunct to finger spelling). One inspector speaking from teaching experience of the use of finger spelling in these circumstances told us that established oral habits had not been undermined.

Professional workers and organisations concerned with the welfare of deaf adolescents and adults

215. Evidence from those concerned with the welfare of deaf adolescents and adults was invited from the National Council of Missioners and Welfare Officers to the Deaf and from a small number of individual officers with experience in both rural and urban areas. A number of welfare workers wrote to us individually in response to our published invitation to submit evidence. In addition we consulted the Royal National Institute for the Deaf and the Scottish Association for the Deaf.

216. The views of the British Deaf and Dumb Association, the British Association of the Hard of Hearing and the National Deaf Children's Society are

referred to later in this Chapter in sections dealing with the evidence of deaf and hard of hearing people and of parents of deaf children. These three bodies are of course vitally concerned with the welfare of the deaf and hard of hearing, but as 'consumers' they represent a special point of view.

217. In considering evidence from professional welfare workers we were anxious to establish, if possible, whether their views related to deaf school leavers generally or whether those with whom they came in contact were not fully representative of the products of the schools. Two witnesses from the National Council of Missioners and Welfare Officers to the Deaf told us that the proportion of school leavers attending clubs and societies for the deaf to which welfare officers are attached varies a good deal from one area to another. But even where young people do not attend clubs regularly they usually turn to Welfare Officers for help on special occasions or in emergencies (which tend to occur far more frequently in the lives of the deaf than among the hearing). As a consequence the witnesses from the National Council thought that very few school leavers do not become known to their local welfare officer or missioner. In view of this we thought that it would be helpful if we could obtain illustrative statistics.

218. Some figures of club membership were provided by one of the two selective secondary schools for pupils with impaired hearing. These related to 36 school leavers over the period July, 1961 to 1965 inclusive. They revealed 27 memberships of social or sports clubs for the hearing as against 39 memberships of similar clubs for the deaf, with a fair degree of multiple membership within each type of club. In addition, eleven of these 36 former pupils were identified as members of both deaf and hearing clubs. Those of us who are head teachers of non-selective schools for pupils with impaired hearing can testify that all our deaf school leavers are known to the welfare officer for the deaf, although this does not necessarily mean that he is well acquainted over a period with all our former pupils.

219. To explore the statistical possibilities further, we considered whether sufficient information could be extracted from published records of numbers of senior deaf pupils and of deaf adults on the registers of handicapped persons maintained by local authorities. Possible methods of comparison are described in Appendix C which also records why we decided to abandon this attempt. In the event therefore it proved impracticable to establish statistically the extent to which welfare workers as a whole know the present generation of deaf adolescents and young people. But there are members of this committee whose experience would lead them to believe that there is little doubt that in most areas of the country these workers do in fact come into contact with the great majority of deaf school leavers, often in situations which give them opportunities for unique insights.

220. **The National Council of Missioners and Welfare Officers to the Deaf** is the national body representing welfare officers for the deaf in Great Britain. We understand that nearly all these officers are members. The Council pointed out that its evidence was not based on research findings since no opportunity had existed for it to undertake relevant research. Its members' regular load of case work precluded this, even among those academically qualified to conduct research. Its evidence was however based on observation of and close contact

with deaf people, including, we understand, a number of orally proficient deaf adults who enjoy the facilities offered by clubs for the deaf and 'the relaxed atmosphere which freedom to use manual methods of communication generates.'

221. As we pointed out in Chapter VIII, the general principles of the Council's evidence were presented as the unanimous view of the entire membership. The first of these principles was full support for the policy of the schools in aiming to prepare deaf pupils to participate naturally in the life of the hearing world since, as the Council put it, the handicap of deaf people is 'not only a matter of communication, but of the formation and cultivation of a human mind into patterns which are consistent to the society in which he lives'. In the experience of the Council this aim is not achieved in the lives of the majority of young deaf people and it believes it to be incapable of achievement, except by a small minority, while present methods of education persist unmodified. The Council believes that the separation of partially hearing from deaf pupils in many schools has high-lighted the poor attainments of the deaf; and welfare officers find the young deaf people whom they meet lacking in initiative and self help, uninterested in further education and disinclined to read.

222. In the light of this experience the second general principle of the Council's evidence was that manual media of communication, which members know to have extended the vocabulary and linguistic powers of young deaf people who have come into their care, should be used in education to supplement and clarify oral communication. The Council envisaged that speech, lipreading, finger spelling and signing (although members were not unanimous on the use of signs) would all play a part in a developed combined mode of communication but that schools would remain predominantly oral in approach.

223. The Council regretted that there appears to exist a prejudice in some educational circles against the use of manual media of communication in this supportive role. It told us that it believes that this prejudice springs from what seems to be an unfounded fear that speech and any other forms of communication are incompatible and also from a tendency to regard manual media as appropriate for the communication of feelings and emotions but not of thought. The Council itself saw the advantage of a combined method as a means by which deaf children would gain ideas, knowledge and language in quantity and quality unattainable by most of them by purely oral methods of learning. It emphasised that deaf adolescents' and adults' deficiencies in understanding and knowledge, which formed the basis of much of the work of missioners and welfare officers, were not simply the result of failure in communication but sprang from a limitation of the grasp of ideas.

224. As to the age at which manual media should be introduced to supplement oral media, the Council told us that its members were not unanimous on this. A minority took the view that finger spelling should be used from the start and discarded when children had acquired sufficient language; but the more general opinion was that all deaf children should be taught orally at first and that finger spelling and signs should be introduced at the teacher's discretion if oral media, unsupported, were seen to be producing inadequate results. Broadly speaking the position of the majority of members of the National Council, as we understood it, was that described in paragraphs 196 and 197, with perhaps emphasis on the use of finger spelling more freely than as a minor adjunct to signs.

225. We invited a small number of *individual welfare officers* to answer specific questions about the integration of the deaf in hearing society, their employment, their social life and leisure time activities, and their ability to cope with normal everyday situations. The evidence of two of these welfare workers, one a chaplain to the deaf and the other a lay worker, was of particular interest because of the varied nature of their experience; and we understand that they represent the views of many of their colleagues. One had been engaged in this work for over thirty years and had held posts in London, in mixed urban and rural areas and in areas which were entirely rural. The experience of the other included a close association, for a recent period of twelve years, with a day school for the deaf and with an audiology clinic to which parents brought young children suspected of deafness. This welfare worker had also been responsible for a youth club attended by deaf adolescents and school children and assisted in running evening classes for the deaf.

226. Neither considered that there was a satisfactory degree of integration of deaf people into hearing society, either at work or in social life. On the one hand the better educated among the younger deaf were often in fields of employment not consonant with their educational attainments; on the other, the majority was separated from normal society by poor language attainments and inability to grasp abstract concepts.

227. Both these workers had found that deaf people generally had insufficient speech and lipreading ability to obtain suitable employment unaided. There was much less difficulty in retaining jobs, partly because deaf people are often in occupations requiring the minimum of verbal instruction; but promotion is very difficult to obtain.

228. On the subject of the contribution of deaf people to society, one of these witnesses said, 'In my experience, it is the younger oral deaf with no manual communication but with such a poor language attainment that lipreading is of only limited use to them, who are able to make the least contribution to the community. Unable to mix with the deaf who communicate manually, either because they have been taught to look on finger spelling and signing with disfavour or because their parents forbid them to do so, they live in a sub-culture on the fringe of the hearing environment. Unlike the less oral deaf who are able to achieve normality for a few hours each week in each other's company, these young people seem to become increasingly conscious of their handicap and their own inferiority. They are usually very dependent upon their families and possible feel incapable of contributing to a wider community of which they are largely ignorant.'

229. As to leisure time activities, both welfare workers said that intellectual pursuits were rare and that very few deaf people read anything other than illustrated papers and magazines. In areas where there is not a convenient club for the deaf or the club does not cater for the needs of young people, younger deaf people tend to band together in groups to go to dances, football matches, the cinema or clubs for the deaf at a considerable distance from their homes.

230. Finally, we were told that by and large the speech and lipreading attainments of average deaf people are not adequate for their ordinary daily needs, beyond very simple ones e.g. shopping. Their vocabulary is not only small but also limited in its range of meanings and mistakes in grammar and syntax are

numerous. The extent to which they can cope was described by one of these witnesses as follows: 'They became adept at going through life without using more verbal communication than necessary. They travel to work by bus or tube by tendering the exact fare, they accomplish much with an expressive face and a nod and a smile; they manage much of their shopping by the use of gesture, and the supermarket has proved an incontestable boon to them. They cope with their routine affairs tolerably successfully, but they are baffled by an income tax return, unable to answer the questions on a national insurance certificate, a form for the insurance or licensing of a car. They require help with a visit to the doctor or a hospital and certainly to arrange a mortgage with a building society or anything appertaining to the law. In short they are likely to require help with any new situation which requires a written answer or brings them into contact with strangers.'

231. **The Royal National Institute for the Deaf and the Scottish Association for the Deaf** are voluntary associations of people concerned to advance the interests of the deaf. Their membership includes workers in many different professions concerned with the deaf, friends and relatives of the deaf and the deaf themselves, but in the main they are associations of hearing people working on behalf of the deaf. The Scottish Association is one of a number of associations affiliated to the Royal National Institute for the Deaf and the organisation as a whole undertakes many activities to increase and disseminate knowledge of deafness and is directly responsible for providing and maintaining a number of services for deaf people.

232. To these and several other bodies with a large and varied membership, we sent a brief questionnaire designed to obtain views on the place, if any, of finger spelling and signing in the education of children with impaired hearing, the children for whom these media might be thought suitable, and the circumstances and manner in which they might be used. We understand that the Royal National Institute for the Deaf deputed the task of answering this questionnaire to an ad hoc sub-committee consisting of an otologist, teachers of the deaf, an independent hard-of-hearing person and welfare officers to the deaf. The answers given by the Scottish Assocation were also prepared by an ad hoc sub-committee and were endorsed by the Association's Executive Committee. In the case of the Scottish Association the ad hoc sub-committee included representatives of the medical and teaching professions, a parent of a deaf child, members of local education authorities and welfare officers to the deaf.

233. The views expressed in the memorandum submitted on behalf of the Royal National Institute for the Deaf were that finger spelling should be introduced during the primary education of deaf pupils and used simultaneously and synchronously with speech. Its purpose would be to accelerate the acquisition of normal language to provide relief from the frustration caused by limited oral communication. There could be a restricted use of individual signs in conjunction with other media of communication, but every endeavour should be made to standardise signs for this purpose. For slow learning deaf children, every use should be made of finger spelling and signing in combination with lipreading and amplified speech. No specific recommendation was made in respect of partially hearing pupils but the authors of the memorandum were of the opinion that partially hearing pupils would benefit from a knowledge and practice of finger spelling in the secondary stage of education.

234. The views of the Scottish Association were somewhat different, but this arose partly because they appeared to distinguish between deaf and partially hearing pupils solely on the basis of degree of hearing loss. However, they did not in any case appear to envisage.that the education of primary school pupils would be by any methods other than oral. It was their view however that by the time a child reached the age of about twelve it should be possible to determine whether he was failing to make progress by purely oral methods and if that were so he should be taught finger spelling as part of a combined method of instruction. The Association thought that this was likely to be necessary for most children with a profound or total hearing loss, but that it might also be necessary for some with a partial hearing loss.

Those concerned with the employment and further education of the deaf

235. Some of the evidence on this subject came from individual welfare officers or missioners and from the National Council of Welfare Officers and Missioners to the Deaf; we have referred to this in paragraphs 220 to 230. In addition, however, we were helped by four youth employment officers in Liverpool, London and Manchester who have special responsibilities in placing deaf school leavers in employment*. These officers agreed to answer questions about media of communication used by the deaf on leaving school and the effect of these on placement, training, adjustment to work and entry upon day release courses. In addition, we conducted a limited enquiry among a group of special schools selected from those known to have experience of placing deaf school leavers in courses of further education and in jobs requiring attendance at day release courses.

236. The youth employment officers reported that speech and lipreading are used (or tried) in their interviews with deaf school leavers, but sometimes the assistance of parents or teachers is needed to establish communication and it may be necessary to resort to writing. Two officers said that the interviews were generally satisfactory although less detailed than those with hearing school leavers because of the limited language ability of the deaf; some can only understand signs. Three officers mentioned that at school leaving age deaf school leavers are using finger spelling and signs to communicate with each other and with friends and parents.

237. It was emphasised that good lipreading ability makes for greater ease in placing a deaf school leaver in employment and that this is also necessary for training on the job. The experience of one officer suggested that placement in a job requiring systematic training was unlikely unless the leaver could lipread well and speak intelligibly; but elsewhere it appeared that sufficient communication for training on the job had been established by demonstration and the use of some signs to supplement lipreading.

238. Generally speaking there appeared to be no serious difficulties in settling at work. Young deaf people seemed to have few changes in employment and certainly no more than young people with normal hearing (see also paragraph 261 (f) below). On the other hand, problems could arise from the employee's limited powers of communication; supervisors sometimes became impatient when

---

* The responsibilities of the youth employment service cease when young workers reach the age of eighteen.

instructions were not understood or when the employee failed to indicate that he had not understood. Where employers not used to deaf work-people were helped in the matter of communication, or the deaf employee was able to make an effort to overcome the difficulty, relationships with employers were reasonably satisfactory. It was pointed out by one officer that deaf employees with poor lipreading ability sometimes preferred to work where there were other deaf employees and that this could conflict with a suitable choice of job.

239. Relationships with work-mates with normal hearing were not without difficulties, but these were often resolved by goodwill. Communication frequently improved as the young deaf worker gained confidence. Sometimes, however, ill-founded suspicions grew in the mind of the young deaf person that his fellow workers were unsympathetic or unfriendly.

240. As to attendance at day release courses, it appeared that boys may be engaged as trainees rather than apprentices if they are likely to find it too difficult to follow group instruction, although they can manage apprenticeships with a large content of practical training. One officer estimated that about one half of deaf school leavers have such limited powers of verbal assimilation that they need instruction by means of signs, a medium of communication not generally available. As a consequence they are limited in choice to less skilled manual employment or work which can be readily taught by visual demonstration. Another significant factor mentioned was that deaf school leavers have difficulty with colloquial as much as with technical language when entering employment or undertaking training or examinations. There was a need for more courses of further education with special assistance from teachers of the deaf.

241. The results of the parallel enquiry we conducted among eight special schools for the deaf should not be taken as necessarily typical since we deliberately approached schools from among those known to make special arrangements for school leavers to take courses of further education and to keep in touch with their leavers. At the same time we do not wish to suggest that other special schools do not concern themselves with further education; we understand that there are efforts on a broad front to increase the educational opportunities of senior pupils and school leavers.

242. At a number of the schools in our enquiry deaf pupils could begin courses of further education at local technical colleges before leaving school. These courses were taken mainly during the day, but there was also attendance at evening classes. In one school over a recent period of three years, one third to one half of school leavers had attended a technical college from the special school. Proportions ranged very widely among the schools in respect of leavers continuing with further education after leaving school.

243. We asked these schools why other leavers did not take opportunities for further education and apart from those replies which related to the nature of the jobs taken, or the attitudes of employers to day release, the reasons given related mainly to lack of ability, interest or determination, and to retardation becoming more apparent when the student could not call upon the help of a teacher of the deaf. Curiously, communication difficulties were mentioned only once as an obstacle to entering upon further education, but it seems probable

that these were implied by some of the more general references to retardation and poor attainments.

244. We also asked questions about the educational and social integration of deaf students in courses at ordinary colleges of further education. In general integration presented few problems in practical work, but difficulties tended to occur in lectures unless a teacher of the deaf was available to help at the lecture and after. Socially, the attitudes of hearing students in the same course ranged from toleration to kindness and friendliness. Where there was inadequate educational and social participation by the deaf, this was mainly because of language difficulties and difficulties of oral communication. Lack of general ability and lack of persistence were mentioned less frequently.

245. As to general social and recreational activities at colleges of further education, most of the replies indicated a non-existent or only a modest degree of participation by deaf students. One school suggested that participation is greater where there are groups of hearing and deaf students in the same college, enabling the deaf students to communicate on two levels and avoid feeling isolated. The reactions of hearing students generally ranged from shyness, through curiosity to eventual understanding and helpfulness.

246. Six of the eight schools indicated that special help is available for deaf students either within the college or from outside it or sometimes from both directions. This help was most often provided by teachers of the deaf, but sometimes by some other person such as a welfare officer. In two cases special help by subject teachers at the college of further education was mentioned.

247. As we have already pointed out, it should not be assumed that the findings of this enquiry can be taken to be generally representative; and we have already referred to the impression of the National Council of Missioners and Welfare Officers to the Deaf that there is a general lack of interest in further education among the great majority of deaf school leavers. At the same time, this limited enquiry suggests that the needs of deaf school leavers for further education are not being neglected.

Deaf and Hard of Hearing Adults
(a) The British Deaf and Dumb Association
248. This voluntary association has a very large membership of deaf adults, including some deaf welfare workers. Hearing people with an interest in or professional concern with the deaf are also members. We understand that the Association has retained the word 'Dumb' in its title not because it is opposed to the aims of oral education but because it does not wish the fundamental problem of the deaf, the difficulty of acquiring spoken language, to be overlooked. Its deaf members include some who are orally proficient. It provides a wide range of social and educational activities, including recreational and cultural courses for young people. Like the Royal National Institute for the Deaf it aims to increase and disseminate knowledge of deafness. The Association has international contacts through its membership of the World Federation of the Deaf and takes part in the organisation of international, interdisciplinary conferences.

249. In paragraph 162, we described the nature of the evidence obtained by the British Deaf and Dumb Association from its deaf members and there is little to

add to our earlier comments. We should make it clear however that the policy of the Association is not to advocate the substitution of manual for oral media of communication in the education of deaf children but to press for the addition of finger spelling and signing to speech and lipreading.

(b) The British Association of the Hard of Hearing

250. The members of this voluntary association are mostly people who lost their hearing, either wholly or in part, after receiving a normal education. We understand however that some members suffered an impairment of hearing in childhood after the age at which speech and language are acquired naturally and that a number of young people with severely impaired hearing which was diagnosed early are now qualifying for membership on the basis of their speech and lipreading ability. These appear to be persons whose auditory training, response to amplified sound and lipreading ability had enabled them to be educated as partially hearing pupils.

251. The aims of the Association include the fostering of social and cultural activities of the hard of hearing, the investigation of problems of deafness, and co-operation with those concerned in the prevention and cure of deafness, the preservation of hearing and the provision of services for the hard of hearing.

252. The evidence of the Association was submitted by its Education Committee and expressed the opinion that for the great majority of children with auditory impairment the aim should be to achieve oral communication so that they can take their place alongside people with normal hearing. In the Association's view, this aim can only be achieved through purely oral methods of education. The use of finger spelling and signing should be reserved for the small minority who do not develop an ability for speech and who should be educated in separate schools, although with arrangements for the transfer of individual pupils between the two types of school according to need. The Association recognised the limitations of lipreading but suggested that these can be overcome by training suitable people to act as 'lip speakers', repeating silently what is said by a speaker, rather on the analogy of an interpreter using finger spelling and signs. The Association suggested that this technique, already in use among adults, could be adopted in schools.

(c) Other deaf adults

(i) *Written evidence*

253. Deaf people of all ages wrote to us either on their own initiative or at the suggestion of their welfare officers or missioners. Some of these correspondents had become deaf after acquiring speech and language naturally but unless age at onset of deafness was stated it was impossible to assess the personal experience which lay behind the evidence. Clearly however there was a wide variety.

254. The majority of our correspondents indicated that they based their views about the education of deaf children on their own experience, some of it relating to adult life, and many felt very strongly that manual media of communication should be used in teaching, although this was not a unanimous view. We cannot claim, of course, that those who wrote to us constitute a representative sample of opinion among deaf adults and for the reasons given in paragraph 166, we consider that the difficulties of obtaining a sample of valid opinion are formidable. While therefore we respect the view that the deaf above all have a right to

be heard in this matter, we would hesitate to interpret the results of surveys of opinion. For our own part, we can do no more than report that a large majority of our deaf correspondents thought that there is a place for finger spelling or signing or both in the education of deaf children; and that there were clear indications that many of these writers were dissatisfied either with their own education or conversely with what they had seen of educational results today, contrasting these with the results of their own education.

(ii) *Oral evidence*

255. We explained in paragraph 165 that our special arrangements for obtaining evidence from the deaf included the taking of oral evidence. The five deaf witnesses who appeared before us in person included a university graduate with a higher degree, an engineering draughtsman, and a technician. The two other witnesses were married women, one of whom was engaged in statistical work in a Government Department. All, except one, were deaf from birth or very early infancy. Four had 'been educated by purely oral methods, but of these one communicated almost entirely by signs or writing. (The signs used by this witness appeared to be based partly on those picked up at school out of class; their esoteric character caused some difficulties in interpretation and in the understanding of our questions put through an interpreter.) The fifth witness had been educated in a school where combined media of communication were used in class. This young man had continued his education after leaving school, studying with the help of correspondence courses, and had obtained G.C.E. passes at O and A level and a City and Guilds qualification. He told us that he had always had great difficulty in lipreading and he communicated with us through an interpreter mainly by finger spelling.

256. Of the three witnesses who communicated fluently by oral means, one had not become deaf until the age of nine but was the child of deaf parents. It was interesting to note that both the other witnesses who were orally proficient at high level and were deaf from birth or early infancy had enjoyed the advantages of individual help and training of an exceptional quality and amount from the very start of their lives. In addition, both had an aptitude for lipreading, which in one case was assisted by amplified sound to exploit a small amount of residual hearing.

257. Nearly all our witnesses placed great emphasis on the need of the deaf to acquire facility in reading and writing and on the need for flexibility in education. To quote one of them: 'I think I was luckier than many other deaf people because I always liked to read. From literature I learned to anticipate social situations and situations of communication—what a speaker was likely to say next.' Speaking later this same witness said: 'If the aim is to prepare children to live in the hearing world, the obvious way is to make the maximum use of speech. But conditions should not be rigid or constricting; there should be a variety of teachers and teaching situations. Teaching should not become mechanical speech training.' On a similar theme another witness said: 'My general comment on education would be that there should be more flexibility so that school life does not consist only of lipreading and learning to listen. Not all deaf children can lipread and only a few can do so effectively. In special cases teachers should be prepared to finger spell or sign or both. Some deaf children have keen minds but because they cannot lipread they make poor progress. I have known of children who have left school unable to read or write effectively.' A third witness,

asked which subject he would have liked to have seen allotted more time in the curriculum, replied: 'English', without a moment's hesitation.

258. We are not suggesting that any one of our witnesses is a 'typical' deaf person; indeed, we were at pains to invite five adults whose individual experiences, problems and achievements would help to give us an insight into a number of different aspects of the life and education of the deaf. We are most grateful to them for describing their personal experiences and views and we have noted the importance which most of them attached to the need for deaf people to have a firm grasp of language and their unanimity that purely oral methods of education are unlikely to be appropriate for all deaf children.

(iii) *A survey*

259. The other part of our special arrangements for obtaining evidence from the deaf consisted of the survey, referred to in paragraph 165 to 168, carried out on our behalf by Miss Brooke-Hughes of the Ministry of Health. This was conducted among young deaf people who left school in the years 1956 to 1965 and who had been maintained by the former London County Council at schools for the deaf in London or elsewhere. They were selected as former pupils who were understood by their schools to have been born with a severe impairment of hearing or to have suffered such an impairment before the age at which speech and language are acquired naturally. This was largely confirmed by the young people interviewed, of whom only three said that they had become deaf at the age of three or later.

260. Invitations to take part in the survey were sent to 150 young people who were believed still to be living in or near London. Letters were returned in 43 cases because the last known addresses were no longer correct. Of the remainder, 42 produced no replies or it proved impossible to contact the young people for interview. A further 13 of those invited said that they were unwilling to take part. Finally, 52 young people (33 men and 19 women) were interviewed, of whom more than half were aged 21 or less. This group was, in a sense, self-selected and we cannot say what reasons prompted those who took part to do so. The interviews were arranged either at clubs for the deaf (15 young people) or at the homes of the young people (37). To save time it had been hoped to arrange a greater number of interviews at clubs, but in spite of the care taken to use direct and simple language in correspondence a number of young people did not appear at the clubs on the evenings fixed for interviews, having failed to understand the connection between agreeing to be interviewed and attending the club.

261. The questions put by the interviewer were mainly designed to obtain facts about media of communication used in various circumstances, including the media of communication which had been used in teaching in the school attended by the young person. 31 of the young people said that they had been taught by speech and lipreading only, while the remaining 21 said that signs, or finger spelling and signs, had been used in addition to speech and lipreading. In addition, the following information was obtained:

(a) Communication with other deaf people

Virtually all the young people said that they communicated with other deaf people by silent speech, lipreading and signs. About half used finger spelling in addition to these media.

(b) Communication with hearing people

The majority said that they would speak when attempting to communicate with a hearing person. Many would, in addition, resort to writing when this appeared necessary. A minority either always used pencil and paper or used them if they were meeting a particular hearing person for the first time. A few who used speech, or speech and writing, also made use of gesture.

(c) Ease of communication with hearing people on leaving school and starting work

Understanding others: a number of young women and one young man said that they understood a lot of what hearing people said. No young woman admitted to understanding nothing but this admission was made by some of the young men. More men than women said that they understood a little. (The interviewer suspected that answers to this question were influenced by differences in attitude between the sexes. The young men seemed to mind much less than the young women about not being understood by hearing people.)

Being understood: more young women than men said that hearing people understood them a lot and very few admitted to not being understood at all, whereas a number of young men made this admission. About half of the numbers of each sex said that hearing people understood them a little. (The interviewer found that more women than men in the survey had been taught by purely oral methods. She pointed out that in deaf oral circles there is a tendency to regard speech shortcomings as 'not clever' and this may have had a bearing on the differences in answers to this question as between the men and women.)

(d) Effect of time upon ease of communication

Most of the young people said that communication had become easier than it had been when they first left school. However, a substantial minority thought that time had had no effect or an adverse effect.

(e) Media of communication used at School

The young people were asked to describe the media of communication used in their education and to say whether they approved or disapproved the use of these media in teaching. Although we were anxious that they should have opportunity to comment on their education, we included these questions with considerable hesitation in view of the reservations which must be made about accuracy of recall and objectivity of view when former pupils of any school are invited to comment upon teaching methods. The young people's answers are summarised in Table VI. We stress the need to interpret the results with caution, not only for the reason we have given but also because we have no means of knowing whether this very small and partly self-selected sample can be regarded as typical.

Table VI: Views of former Pupils on Media of Communication used in their Education

Medium used in teaching	Total number of pupils	Numbers	
		(a) *Approving*	(b) *Disapproving*
Oral	31	10	21
Oral plus manual	21	19	2*
Total	52	29	23

* These two young people had been taught by a combination of speech, lipreading and signs, and thought that the addition of finger spelling would have been helpful.

(f) Employment

The survey revealed that frequent job changing was very rare. Nearly half the young people had been in the same job since leaving school and few had changed their job more than once. Pay and ability to get on well with work-mates appeared the most important aspects to the young people. Dissatisfaction appeared rarely to be felt once a job was obtained, although a few young people were aiming for something better. In the case of those interviewed at home, the status of the young person's job appeared often more important to his parents than to himself.

(g) Points arising indirectly from the survey

1. The survey revealed differences of approach and attitude in the young people which appeared to be related to the schools they attended to the extent that the interviewer felt able, after some conversation with a young person, to guess correctly the name of the school he or she had attended. Ease of communication varied tremendously and some who had the greatest difficulty in making themselves understood were the most intolerant of those who did not use speech and lipreading.

2. In the home visits the interviewer was able to see only one deaf person unaccompanied, although 31 were aged 21 to 26. Frequently both parents were present and much time and explanation were required to create opportunities for the young person to answer the questions unprompted or uncontradicted. The survey suggested that overprotectiveness of parents may extend into the adult life of those handicapped by deafness and be disadvantageous to the deaf person. We shall have more to say about this and its bearing on the guidance of parents in Chapter XIII.

Parents of deaf children

(a) The National Deaf Children's Society

262. This Society is the only voluntary body in the United Kingdom concerned exclusively in promoting the welfare of deaf children. Its membership consists largely of parents of deaf children but also includes many teachers of the deaf, otologists and other workers concerned professionally with deaf children. It provides an advisory service for parents and is concerned to enlarge public knowledge of the problems of deaf children and to promote relevant educational as well as medical research.

263. The evidence of the Society was prepared by its Education Committee whose members include both teachers of the deaf and parents of deaf children. The view expressed in its memorandum was that there was a limited place for finger spelling for children without oral ability. Apart from education, there are occasions of emotional atmosphere when finger spelling may be the only safe means of ensuring that a child understands an urgent message. Finger spelling could be used in education in combination with lipreading and speech to explain difficult words or phrases, but the child should not have to follow both simultaneously. It was also the view of the Society that signing is seldom grammatical, but there is a place for it in the education of late starters, such as some immigrant children with no written and spoken language background, and for some older children who have failed to benefit from purely oral training.

(b) Individual parents

264. A small number of parents of deaf children wrote to us in response to our published invitation to submit evidence. The children of some of them were still at school, others had left very recently and some were grown up. Since their opinions, which covered a wide range of views, were mainly related to individual experiences in which many unknown factors must have operated it was impossible to evaluate most of them. For this reason we considered whether it was practicable to conduct a survey among parents of media of communication actually used by their children in various circumstances and other relevant facts, relating these to ascertainable information about age at onset of deafness, age when hearing loss was detected, degree and type of hearing loss, early training and so on. Unfortunately the difficulties of carrying out such a survey in the time available to us proved insurmountable, but we hope that it may be possible for this to be undertaken at some time in the future as a means of throwing more light on the media of communication of deaf children outside school and the processes of communication in very early childhood as between parents (especially mother) and child.

Medical witnesses and non-medical clinicians

265. We invited evidence from consultants in otology, psychiatry, paediatrics and neurology and from medical officers of the Department of Education and Science and a large local education authority. In addition we approached non-medical clinicians with experience of communication problems in children and also consulted two phoneticians. To all these witnesses we put the single question: 'From your own experience what (medical) evidence, if any, throws light on the subject of the Committee's study?'

266. These witnesses were not able to refer us to any evidence with experimental backing which they considered to be directly relevant to our terms of reference. One, indeed, expressed the view that it would be extremely difficult to produce either medical or non-medical evidence for or against the place of finger spelling or signing in the education of the deaf in view of the difficulty of establishing any convincing or satisfactory controls to assess the relative value of manual and oral media of communication. Not the least important part of this difficulty lay in the presence of so many variables in the ability or inability of deaf children to be taught to communicate by speech. However, although these witnesses could not provide objective evidence directly bearing on our study, most of them were able to help us with observations from experience and to offer considered opinions based on these observations. A theme which ran through much of their evidence was the vital importance to children of having a means of communication and the power of self-expression. In the words of one, '. . . . literally any means of communication is better than no means at all'.

267. Many of these witnesses were well acquainted with cases of children with impaired hearing who had not learned to communicate with intelligible speech and whose command of language was very inadequate. The Principal Medical Officer of the Department of Education and Science pointed out that many children who would have responded well to oral methods of education in schools for the deaf were no longer admitted to these schools but were taught instead in special schools and classes for the partially hearing. In his view it may well have been that in the past the pupils in schools for the deaf who had usable

hearing for speech masked the inadequate achievement of the others. Many of those now remaining in schools for the deaf seemed to be children who found it difficult or impossible to acquire intelligible speech and whose language development was seriously retarded. Evidence of this had emerged from a survey of senior pupils reported in 'The Health of the School Child, 1962 and 1963'[1]. (See also paragraph 18). While many of these children may not have had the benefit of early diagnosis and special educational treatment, these appeared to him not to be the only factors since some younger children now in schools for the deaf also seemed to find it difficult to acquire intelligible speech and to develop language adequately. The Principal Medical Officer thought it inevitable that with a rapid expansion of separate services for partially hearing pupils schools for the deaf would be admitting children who presented very difficult problems.

268. Evidence from some of our medical witnesses dealt with the incidence and nature of emotional disturbance among the deaf. They were unable to give us statistical evidence of the incidence of maladjustment in the general population of deaf children, nor was there evidence relating maladjustment to particular media of communication. There were however studies of incidence in selected groups of deaf children and adolescents.[2] The Principal Medical Officer of the Department of Education and Science referred to the common impression which seemed to exist that the incidence of emotional disturbance is lower among deaf children than among children with normal hearing. He thought that this impression might be partly the result of a general tendency not to refer deaf children to child guidance clinics because of difficulties of communication. Knowledge of the nature and causes of maladjustment among children with impaired hearing would be gained from the experience of the new school for seriously disturbed deaf and partially hearing pupils* established by the Royal National Institute for the Deaf.

269. Our attention was drawn to the strong indications that in the adult population maladjustment illnesses are more prevalent among the profoundly deaf than among hearing people, certainly in so far as patients receiving treatment in hospital are concerned.[3] It was the view of one of our medical witnesses that if deaf patients had possessed a more mature language ability, the acute crises leading to hospital admission might not have arisen in a number of cases. He maintained that if this view were tenable, and there were indications that it was, then everything possible should be done to assist language development from an early age in order to counteract the tendency to the lower threshold of breakdown which so often occurs among the deaf.

270. While some of the doctors and non-medical clinicians we invited to submit evidence felt unable to express an opinion based on experience, the majority of those we approached thought that there might well be a need for non-oral media of communication for some deaf children. In the view of some witnesses, this might be limited to specific categories of children e.g. those with additional defects. One witness with wide experience among deaf children and adults urged that controlled experimental studies should be started as soon as possible to establish whether children who had not made progress when taught orally could be helped by manual media of communication and to find out ways by

---

* Larchmoor, Stoke Poges, Buckinghamshire.

which children unlikely to make progress orally could be discovered as early as possible. Another drew attention to the need for further research into causes of deafness and into ways of relating methods of overcoming the defect to its cause. Reference was also made to the presence in schools for the deaf of children with communication problems not arising from deafness. It was felt that there is a lack of adequate diagnostic facilities and that stress should be placed on a multi-disciplinary approach. It was essential to arrive at a full diagnosis in these cases as early as possible since not only might the problems of these children be intensified by purely oral methods of education but it was essential to avoid complicating the problems of educational methods for deaf pupils by the presence in the same school of children with different handicaps requiring different treatment.

271. To sum up, the evidence from this category of witnesses could be expressed as a belief that present results appeared to justify an empirical approach to communication in the education of some deaf children and a recognition that those responsible for education needed the help of better diagnostic and assessment services and of further extensions of medical knowledge.

REFERENCES

1.

Survey of children born in 1947 who were in schools for the deaf in 1962–63, The Health of the School Child 1962 and 1963, The Report of the Chief Medical Officer of the Department of Education and Science, pp. 60 to 71; H.M. Stationery Office, price 12s. 6d. net.

2. D. C. Kendall

The mental development of young deaf children. Unpublished Thesis, University of Manchester, 1953; and in *Educational guidance and the deaf child,* ed. Ewing. Manchester University Press, 1957.

Behaviour problems in young deaf children. The Teacher of the Deaf, 1951, vol. XLIX, pp. 103–108.

The contribution of parent guidance to the mental health of deaf children, article 56 in *The Modern Educational Treatment of Deafness, Report of the International Conference held in Manchester,* 1958 ed. Ewing. Manchester University Press, 1960.

Edna S. Levine

Psychological aspects and problems of early profound deafness. American Annals of the Deaf, 1958, Vol. 103, p. 324.

The Psychology of deafness. New York, Columbia University Press, 1960.

Youth in a soundless world. New York, Columbia University Press, 1956.

L. J. Murphy

The assessment of the abilities of deaf children. Unpublished Thesis, University of Manchester, 1952.

K. P. Murphy

A survey of the intelligence and abilities of 12 year old deaf children. Unpublished Thesis, University of Manchester, 1956; and in The Child who does not talk, *Clinics in developmental medicine,* 13. Heinemann, 1964.

J. D. Rainer,
K. Z. Altshuler,
F. J. Kallmann,
W. Edwards Denning.

Family and mental health problems in a deaf population. Department of Medical Genetics, New York State Psychiatric Institute, Columbia University, New York, 1963.

The *psychiatric needs of the deaf;* Report of a working party of The Royal Medico-Psychological Association, ed. G. O'Gorman, Royal Medico-Psychological Association, 1962.

3. John C. Denmark   *Mental illness and early profound deafness,* Brit. J. Med. Psychol., 1966, 39, 117.

Chapter XII. Survey of Main Trends of Opinion and Main Areas of Disagreement in Evidence

272. The views described in the three preceding Chapters range widely and are concerned with children with a variety of different characteristics at all stages of education from the nursery class to the college of further education. Opinions have been expressed which are shared across professional boundaries; and differences of opinion exist both within professions and as between individuals in different professions. Although there are no major issues on which opinion divides along the frontiers of professions, there are views which tend to command majority support in one profession but not in another. The opinions recorded have no doubt been influenced in a number of ways: by the history of education of deaf children in this country, by the way in which the full-time professional education of teachers of the deaf has developed with special emphasis on oral methods and technical advance, and by knowledge gained from experience in special but limited fields. The existence of arrangements for in-service professional training in two of the professions mainly concerned may also have resulted in some crystallisation of views within them. For these reasons we believe that there are advantages in having indicated the kinds of experience and expertise associated with the conclusions which witnesses put before us. Divergencies of view seem not to be very numerous or entirely irreconcilable. We hope that by bringing together opinions in a comprehensive account the divisive factors will be seen to be fewer than was thought and the way will be prepared for further constructive discussion. It may be helpful if we now summarise the main trends of opinion and areas of disagreement which emerged from the evidence as a whole. Our comments and recommendations are in the final chapter which follows.

2 Aims of education

73. There is general agreement that the principal aims in educating children with impaired hearing should be to enable them to realise their full potential and so far as possible take their place in society in due course as literate adults with whole personalities which they can express through generally understood media of communication. The accomplishment of these aims requires efforts of mind and heart from the children themselves and from their parents and teachers which incomparably exceed those demanded in many other spheres of life. There is no dispute that in the education of deaf pupils achievement too often falls very short of what is desired or that there are special difficulties in establishing a compatability of aims. Communication is the fundamental need of every child and to reconcile ways of meeting this need with longer term aims sometimes presents serious problems in teaching deaf children.

Partially hearing and deaf pupils—the main points of view

274. Few of our witnesses suggested that children who are properly regarded as partially hearing should be taught by methods which are not purely oral. The differences of opinion centred almost entirely around deaf pupils and can be expressed in terms of three main positions. First there is the view that few deaf children make adequate progress if methods of education which are exclusively oral are used throughout school life; that this is so is demonstrated by results which can be clearly seen in the lives of many young deaf people. Secondly, there

is the opposite view, supported by evidence of outstanding achievement by some deaf children and young people; the fact that attainments are not generally higher can be attributed to failure in applying the principles of a purely oral method of education at a sufficiently early stage or with adequate zeal. Thirdly, there is the view, which was put to us by some witnesses with wide experience, that it is possible to concentrate attention on media of communication to the neglect of other factors in education which may, in practice, have a more significant influence on results.

Virtually no purists

275. With very few exceptions (referred to at the beginning of Chapter X), adherents of all three main points of view were unanimous that there should be no return to the education of deaf children by entirely silent methods. And there were no witnesses who wished to claim that exclusively oral methods are appropriate for all deaf children at all stages of education; but it was generally agreed that there are stages at which oral methods alone are likely to produce the most satisfactory results irrespective of the aptitudes and characteristics of individual children. Some witnesses, the majority, considered that this was so at least in the early stages when the foundations of language and speech are being laid. Others believed that precisely because these stages are so critical there should be a carefully devised supplementation of oral media of communication with finger spelling or signs to assist in the establishment of correct patterns of language; these props might well be discarded later as children grew towards the stage at which they would no longer be able to lean on them in ordinary life.

Deaf children with additional disabilities

276. Deaf children with specific additional disabilities were perhaps those whose problems seemed to call for similar solutions in the minds of the greatest number of our witnesses. There was general agreement that not many slow learning children suffering from a disability causing impaired intellectual functioning, or from a speech and language disorder unrelated to deafness, were likely to make progress by purely oral methods of education unless advances in medical knowledge pointed to ways in which these could be effectively adapted. And among witnesses with professional experience of the education of deaf children it was generally thought that finger spelling, both in execution and reading, was as difficult for those with additional disabilities as speech and written language. This was underlined in medical evidence where it was pointed out that the additional disabilities of some of these children precluded the possibility of linguistic development. It seemed to be the general view that in communicating with and teaching these children it was often necessary to supplement speech with gestures, simple signs and mime. It must of course be remembered that there are children who may have specific additional disabilities who are thought of by those dealing with them simply as being deaf.

Older deaf children with no additional disabilities

277. It was in respect of deaf pupils with no recognised additional disability severely affecting their learning, who had passed the primary stage of education

or completed a major part of it, that divergencies of opinion were the most numerous. These were between:—

(a) those witnesses who considered that the continued application of purely oral methods was the right course and those who believed that these methods could not keep pace with the demands of developing children for new language and information;

(b) advocates of particular types of combined media of communication (see Chapter X);

(c) those witnesses who considered it essential to separate children not taught by purely oral methods and those who saw no need for this or thought it undesirable; and

(d) those who considered that it would be appropriate to introduce finger spelling or signs or both at a particular fixed stage of the education of all children thought likely to benefit and those who considered that within this group, decisions about timing would have to vary as between individual children. A further refinement of this argument was concerned with the use of different combinations of media at different stages of education.

The influence of manual media on oral proficiency and linguistic development
278. Another major controversy surrounded the question whether the use of finger spelling and signs, or either of these separately, interferes with the development of proficiency in oral communication. There is a strong body of opinion which believes that this is so, if only because the use of manual media reduces both time available for the practice of oral skills and the incentives to speak, lipread and listen. Another reason given is that a non-linguistic means of communication, such as signing, interferes with linguistic development. An equally strong body of opinion maintains that proficiency in oral communication can only develop from a sound knowledge of language and fluency in its use. It argues that although lipreading can be taught from the early stages of speech and language development it cannot be effective outside the range of known language. Any means which promotes linguistic development, as finger spelling or signs are held to do in combination with other media, must therefore indirectly influence ability and fluency in oral communication by enlarging the area of effective lipreading and speech.

The non-linguistic character of signing
279. A major point on which there was general agreement was that signing as commonly used at present among deaf adults and, even more, signing as it develops spontaneously among deaf children, are non-linguistic media of communication. Those who recommended the use of signs in education wish to see them standardised and, if not systematised, then used sparingly in ways which would not interfere with the development of normal language.

Chapter XIII. Our Views and Recommendations

Part One

Aims and their implications

280. We have deliberately reserved a statement of our views and recommendations until the closing chapter of this Report. We believe that opinions both for and against the use of manual media of communication in the education of children with impaired hearing have been sincerely expressed to us on the basis of experience but it is our impression that in the past opinions have often been offered too readily without full examination or reflection upon the many factors involved or sufficient regard to the validity and relevance of the experience upon which opposing points of view are based. Preconceptions and prejudices seem to have obscured the issues. Sometimes, we suspect, the debate has continued simply because of an unrecognised confusion of terms. As we have already indicated, ambiguities proliferate in this field. Unnecessary argument is bound to follow if, for example, the term 'impaired hearing' is used by some people to denote a limited and by others the full range of possible hearing handicap; or if 'manualism' can mean either communication by finger spelling and signing alone or the combination of these media with speech and lipreading. We believe that the measure of agreement which in fact exists has been masked by these factors.

281. We hope that we have avoided the pitfalls and that our analysis of evidence and opinions has clarified some of the issues. Our Report is very largely a report of opinions but, as we pointed out in paragraph 163, carefully weighed opinion can give many helpful indications of the directions in which research may be required.

Aims

282. In paragraph 273, we summarised our witnesses' stated aims in the education of children with impaired hearing. These were to enable the children to realise their full potential and as far as possible take their place in society in due course as literate adults with whole personalities which they can express through generally understood media of communication. There is likely to be little disagreement with these aims and we ourselves subscribe to them. At the same time we would emphasise that they represent high aspirations which are not fully realised even by some children with normal hearing. No-one who is concerned in the up-bringing or education of children with impaired hearing can fail to be aware of the qualifications and reservations which have to be made in practice. In the nature of the problem of congenital or early hearing impairment of any degree of severity, it is only in a few cases that any educational method will lead to a full attainment of all these aims. We believe that it is important for the happiness of children that this should be understood and that neither they nor their parents should be given unrealistic expectations or be subject to unrealistic demands.

Implications of aims for partially hearing pupils

283. In Chapter I we explained the basis on which a distinction is made between deaf and partially hearing pupils. It follows from the nature of this distinction,

relating as it does to speech and language development, that partially hearing pupils by definition are children who are more closely approaching an attainment of some of the aims set out above than are children who are classified as deaf. We have received no evidence which would suggest that a full attainment would be more likely if finger spelling or signing were added to the oral media through which these children are at present taught. In view of the great advances which we know are being made in the education of partially hearing pupils and their growing participation in the educational and social activities of children with normal hearing, we do not propose to recommend research or experimentation with manual media in the education of these pupils.

284. There are of course a number of young children, particularly those with severe hearing losses, whose ultimate classification is uncertain. After a prolonged period of special educational treatment some prove capable of continuing their education as partially hearing pupils. We do not exclude children whose ultimate classification is uncertain from the possible scope of research. Our remarks so far have referred only to children whose speech and language development and use of residual hearing have begun to indicate the possibility that they may be classified as partially hearing pupils.

Implications of aims for deaf pupils

285. We have said that it is inherent in the problem of severe early hearing impairment that a full attainment of every aim is likely only in a few cases, irrespective of methods. Should the aims perhaps be modified for deaf pupils? Provided that aims are not unrealistically interpreted and applied, we think it right that they should be ambitious. We propose to examine their implications more closely.

286. Helping deaf pupils to realise their full potential is an unambiguous aim. The difficulty lies in assessing the potential of individual children and measuring their attainments in relation to it. Although the potential intellectual ability of deaf children can to some extent be assessed, it is not possible at present to estimate their potential linguistic ability nor are there satisfactory standardised tests of linguistic attainment appropriate to the deaf. If empirical approaches to teaching methods are to be adopted, teachers will need more help in objective assessment.

287. The second part of our aims relates to the preparation of children to take their place in society as literate adults with whole personalities which they can express through generally understood media of cummunication. Many interpretations of this aim are possible. It is not incompatible with the concept of a non-oral adult living in a community of the deaf and making contact with the rest of society through the media of reading and writing. But this is not what most people are likely to have in mind. The head of St. Mary's School, Cabra, explaining the school's decision to introduce oral methods, said: '.... it was felt, at Cabra, that the deaf child needed a more effective preparation for life in a hearing world which was becoming daily more complicated. Signs merely fitted the deaf adult for life in a silent community and no such community existed in Ireland—outside the Cabra School.' In modern society the spoken word increasingly takes over from the written. It would be difficult to maintain that a person whose sole means of communication is by writing is effectively integrated. We doubt whether this could be maintained even of a person who

comprehends adequately by lipreading but is dependent upon writing as a substitute for speech. On the other hand, to interpret the aim as implying oral communication which is as easy and fluent as normal conversation seems to us unrealistic. Even the most brilliant oralists among the deaf cannot overcome their handicap entirely. Our own view is that the aim should be to achieve some degree of effective oral communication—and we have in mind not only intelligibility but content—while recognising that oral communication may at times need to be supplemented by reading and writing and even by finger spelling*. This seems to us a reasonable level of integration with hearing society for teachers to have before them as an aim for those deaf children whose handicap is not complicated by additional disabilities. Media of communication which are not linguistic should not of course be neglected; the value of these was pointed out in paragraph 67.

Are the aims attained or attainable?

288. There is no doubt that the attainments of many pupils leaving schools for the deaf fall very short of aims as we have modestly interpreted them. This was clear from our evidence and has been demonstrated in investigations. School leavers are frequently deficient not only in oral ability but also in written language and in knowledge gained through language. As a consequence, their place in hearing society is often insecure and peripheral.

289. In the evidence of members of the University staffs responsible for training teachers of the deaf we noted that certain pre-conditions of progress by oral methods were mentioned as seeming to be more important than others. These were early detection and assessment of hearing impairment; the skilled guidance of parents and the auditory training of young children; consistently good oral teaching in school; and close and continuing co-operation between home and school (paragraph 206). If adequate progress is dependent upon these factors we must look at certain underlying assumptions before we can be satisfied that they point to a way by which all deaf children can be sufficiently helped.

290. These assumptions are that there will be comprehensive services in every area for the early detection and assessment of hearing impairment and a universal availability of expert guidance to parents both in the pre-school period and later. For those purposes additional demands must be made upon medical and supplementary professions and there must be a substantially enlarged teaching force. Furthermore, if consistently good oral teaching is to be given, teachers must not only be highly trained but must also be possessed of uniformly high teaching skills. Finally, the assumption must be made that parents are both willing and able to co-operate with the various medical and educational services at every stage of their children's lives.

291. To the pre-conditions of progress by oral methods mentioned in the evidence of the University staffs, we ourselves would add the full diagnosis and assessment as early as possible of other disabilities which may affect learning; good language teaching; and an adequate range of opportunities for further

---

* The Guide movement awards a badge called 'Friend for the Deaf' which among methods of communication with the deaf may include a test for proficiency in the manual alphabet. A similar test is included among those for the Duke of Edinburgh's award. Finger spelling is also taught in some police forces.

education. For the first of these—the differential diagnosis of complex disabilities—there must be a wider availability of medical and psychological services staffed by specialists in a number of fields, including e.g. paediatric neurology, child psychiatry and educational and clinical psychology. There are at present general shortages of child psychiatrists and psychologists and very few indeed who have a knowledge of deafness and the ability to communicate with deaf children. In the whole of England and Wales there are not more than about half a dozen paediatric neurologists. To satisfy our second and third preconditions, further implications for the supply and training of teachers will have to be faced and it may well be necessary to consider the need for systematic curriculum studies both in language teaching and subject courses.

292. We fully endorse the views of those who urge major extensions of all the services involved. We believe that every effort should be made to work towards this end in the shortest possible time and that the possible need for curricular reform should be thoroughly investigated. Having said this, we are bound to state explicitly that what we have been describing is an educational system which is apparently dependent for general effectiveness at a modest level not only upon extensions of great magnitude in its own staffing, and in the staffing of other even more hard-pressed services, but also upon the unflagging co-operation of all parents throughout their children's school lives. We do not believe that it is realistic to regard such a system as completely viable. We have no doubt that improvements can and will be made and that as a result more deaf children than at present will be helped to attain good standards. But equally we have no doubt that in the foreseeable future there will always be some children for whom conditions will remain seriously imperfect.

What are the other possibilities?

293. Alternatives have been presented to us which might be described respectively as preventive and remedial. The first would involve the adoption of a new or modified approach to teaching from the earliest stage of education in the belief that a realistic appraisal of present and future situations calls for radical measures. The second would involve a rescue operation for those children who fail to make adequate progress in present circumstances. The use of manual media of communication might be the instrument for either of these measures and this of course is the central issue before us. We must say straightaway that there is no factual evidence of scientific validity enabling us to make a recommendation in that sense in respect of either preventive or remedial measures. Furthermore we must accept that some factors which contribute to failures in the use of oral methods would also work against a system in which manual media of communication played a part. Skilful teaching is but one example of a pre-requisite of success under any educational system.

294. These considerations were uppermost in the minds of some of our witnesses but we were also presented with a great weight of experienced opinion which favours the use of manual media of communication for some deaf children. Although this opinion is divided on the question of the numbers and type of deaf children likely to be involved, its unanimity on the general principle is important, representing as it does the policies of the professional body of which the great majority of teachers of the deaf are members and of the comparable body to which belong virtually all welfare officers to the deaf. The view that

there is a place for manual media for some deaf children was supported in the evidence of all our witnesses. In a number of overseas countries the same view is held and in some instances is being tested by enquiry and investigation. We recommend that studies should be undertaken in this country to determine whether or not and in what circumstances the introduction of manual media would lead to improvement in the education of deaf children.

Part Two

Research and Investigation

295. The scope for research is wide but resources of manpower and money are not unlimited. The projects which are discussed in paragraphs 300 to 319 below cannot all be undertaken concurrently, nor is it desirable to attempt this since the initiation of some is dependent upon the completion of others. Nevertheless, we hope that it will be possible, where this is appropriate, to undertake a number concurrently and to maintain a continuous programme, bringing the results of research regularly before the schools. For this purpose we recommend that the Department of Education and Science establish without delay an informal consultative body composed of people with knowledge and experience in this highly specialised field of education to advise the Department on the design of research proposals submitted to it, on the initiation of discussions with Universities and other research establishments, and on measures to bring the results of research to the notice of schools.

296. In addition, we hope that the Department will invite the Schools Council for the Curriculum and Examinations to consider the need for promoting and supporting research and development in this field.

297. Our suggestions for research and investigation do not include fundamental research into e.g. the causes of deafness or the nature of specific speech and language disorders. Extensions of knowledge in these fields is essential to progress in the special educational treatment of children with impaired hearing but these are areas of medical and psychological research extending beyond our terms of reference which will require close and continuing study over many years. Some of our own proposals involve long-term studies on which we hope that work can be started as soon as possible. While stressing the urgent need for consultative machinery, we believe that the inception of a research programme should not wait upon its establishment.

298. The planning of research and the making of educational decisions about individual children are greatly facilitated if adequate case records are kept. A standard form of school medical record (Form 10M, Department of Education and Science) is in use, but not all schools are provided with adequate information and some appear not to make full use of information provided. We recommend that local education authorities and non-maintained schools for the deaf and partially hearing (including independent schools used by local education authorities) should consider to what extent existing forms of record and sources of information are adequate for the purpose of educational decisions in respect of individual children and should notify the Department of Education and Science of any major inadequacies which they have experienced. We also recommend that the Department should consult with these bodies on the adoption of appropriate and adequate school records.

299. We now set out our recommendations for research studies and other investigations.

300. The enquiry reported in Chapter VI was inevitably superficial and we believe that it would be of great value to teachers if more detailed information were generally available about such matters as the internal organisation of schools, teaching methods, amount of amplifying equipment and extent of its use, and criteria for the selection of pupils within a school for whom special measures, including the use of combined media of communication, are considered necessary. A comprehensive survey on these lines would make heavy demands on manpower, but we hope that a phased operation may soon begin which would lead to the regular publication of survey reports on samples of schools. These schools would, of course, be unnamed.

301. In addition more detailed studies are required which might be undertaken as the subject of a research degree. We have in mind the need for planned observations of methods used by individual teachers in the organisation of their classrooms, their interaction with pupils and the effect on the pupils linguistically, emotionally and socially. Studies of this kind would require very careful preparation to ensure that the individual teachers constituted the variable factors and that other factors were held constant.

DEVISING MEASURES OF LINGUISTIC ATTAINMENT

302. The introduction of manual media of communication in the education of deaf children is often justified by those who decide to use these media as a means of combating linguistic retardation. Tests of linguistic attainment appropriate for deaf children are not available to assist teachers who feel the need to introduce these media or to adopt other special measures. We consider that standardised tests should be devised of language structures and vocabulary, including semantic range, appropriate to deaf children of different ages to assist teachers in the planning of language teaching.

STUDIES OF INDIVIDUAL CHILDREN
Factors favourable or adverse to the development of oral communication

303. A detailed study is needed of individual deaf pupils to determine which factors or particular combination of factors from among those discussed in Chapter V have a favourable or adverse influence upon the development of ability in oral communication, and whether other significant factors are involved. Children making satisfactory progress, judged by both the intelligibility and content of their oral communication, should be compared with children who, by the same criteria, are not making satisfactory progress. Children should be selected for whom comprehensive case histories are available or can be reliably compiled and these should include detailed accounts of the teaching each child has received. Psychiatric and psychological assessments will be needed. The progress of the children should be followed up over a period of years, during which records should be kept of teaching methods and programmes used. We would suggest that the survey period should extend from a point mid-way through the junior school to school leaving age, and that there should be regular publication of interim results. A pilot study, which need involve only a

small number of children, could be started quite quickly. The retrospective investigation and current assessments of individual children with which it would begin would themselves be likely to produce results of interest to the schools.

The conditions and effects of pre-school training and parent guidance

304. We suggest that there should be started concurrently a longitudinal study concerned specifically with the effects of pre-school training and parent guidance. Unlike the previous study, which would be partly retrospective, this investigation would select for long-term study a number of very young pre-school children, preferably at the stage of diagnosis of hearing impairment. The aim would be to observe the effects of various kinds and amounts of early training and parent guidance and of none. (Although this appears to raise ethical problems, there are, we understand, parts of the country which have great difficulty because of staff shortages in providing and maintaining these services on a systematic basis; these difficulties seem likely to continue for some time. Clearly, however, no child or his parents would be deprived of services for experimental purposes.)

305. Three groups of children would be involved in this study: those who for one reason or another receive little or no early training and whose parents are either unable or unwilling to avail themselves of expert guidance; those who receive pre-school training but whose parents are unable to act in accordance with expert advice offered to them; and those who receive training and whose parents co-operate effectively with the guidance services.

306. A survey of detailed practice in parent guidance and pre-school training will be a necessary part of this study. It could take as its starting point the survey, now being conducted by H.M. Inspectors, of the organisation of peripatetic teaching services for children with impaired hearing; we understand that a report will be published in due course.

Deaf children of deaf parents; effects of the early use of manual media upon later linguistic development

307. The third group of children in the previous study (see paragraph 305) should be matched with a group of young children of deaf parents who use manual media in communicating with their children; and the later achievements of these two groups should be compared. This would be a longitudinal study with the same aims of those of the investigation carried out in the United States of America by Dr. Jack Birch and Dr. E. Ross Stuckless, but it would be designed to control the additional variable factor to which we referred in paragraph 155.

308. As part of this and the previous study we hope that it will be possible to enlist the co-operation of parents in describing in some detail the media of communication actually used by their children in various circumstances outside school and the communication processes in very early childhood between parents and child. (See paragraph 264).

Deaf children with additional disabilities: an investigation of diverse methods of developing communication

309. Witnesses drew our attention to indications of a growing number of children with additional or special disabilities in schools for the deaf. Many of these children are slow learning and some suffer from severe disorders which grossly

97

retard or even preclude linguistic development (paragraphs 184, 185 and 276). It is clear that improved facilities are needed not only for differential diagnosis but also for educational assessment as a continuing process. Some special schools already exist which cater exclusively for deaf pupils with additional disabilities and as knowledge of these problems grows it seems likely that further specialised provision will be made. In the meantime we hope that schools for the deaf will, so far as possible, make separate arrangements within school for those children with the most severe communication difficulties and maintain records of any experimental methods which may be used in teaching and of the results obtained. In a few schools we recommend that systematic experimental work be undertaken, in co-operation with interdisciplinary teams including psychiatrists and psychologists, to assess the effects of a planned teaching programme involving the use of signs, natural gesture and mime.

Social and emotional development in relation to communication

310. The inter-relationship between social and emotional development and various kinds of communication is not clear. A number of hypotheses, some of which conflict need to be tested, e.g. that satisfactory social and emotional development is dependent upon ease of oral communication; that frustration arising from the difficulties of lipreading and listening may be exacerbated in certain types of personality (see paragraph 92) and lead to emotional deterioration which could have been prevented by the use of finger spelling or signing; that measures necessary to attain satisfactory levels of oral ability involve relationships of such closeness between deaf children and hearing adults, especially parents but also teachers and welfare workers, and of such dependence on the part of the children, as to distort the development of personality (c.f. paragraph 261(g)2, where we noted indications from a survey of young deaf adults of over-protectiveness of parents extending into the adult life of the deaf). This is a complex area of study in which it is necessary to identify the influence of factors other than media of communication on social and emotional development. For this reason we suggest that further surveys on the lines of that reported in paragraphs 259–261 should be undertaken in the first place. These should be followed by studies in depth of selected aspects and the conclusions should be taken into account in guidance given to parents and in the professional training of teachers and welfare workers.

EFFECTS OF COMBINING ORAL AND MANUAL MEDIA

Finger spelling: its early use in the U.S.S.R.: a study of possible applications in this country

311. Our study of reports from sources in the U.S.S.R. and elsewhere and the evidence given to us by officers of the Department of Education and Science leave us in no doubt that Russian methods of teaching speech and language to deaf children present a challenge which cannot be ignored. At the same time we recognise the advance made in recent years in this country, which has resulted in greatly improved attainments in speech and language of many children whose residual hearing has been exploited by early training and who have been taught by purely oral methods. We are unanimously of the opinion that any proposal to modify current practices in the teaching of young children with impaired hearing would require the most careful consideration, should be based upon carefully controlled studies and should not involve the denial of amplified

sound to any child whom it would benefit. A major aim of any such study would be to establish whether a teaching method designed for use with the Russian language is adaptable for use with the English language.

312. Accordingly, we recommend that a study of Russian methods should be carried out in co-operation with a British University by an appropriate team. The aims of the study would be:

   (a) to establish whether, prima facie, there are grounds for the conclusion that the methods used in the U.S.S.R. are adaptable for use with the English language;

   (b) to consider how best a controlled experiment could be carried out in this country to determine the suitability of these methods for use with the English language;

   (c) to make recommendations as to the children who might be included in such an experiment, with special reference to types and degrees of hearing impairment; and

   (d) to prepare the outline of a design for such an experiment.

Finger spelling: the Danish mouth-hand system: a study of possible applications in this country

313. Concurrently, if possible, with studies of the Russian method, we recommend that the feasibility should be considered of a controlled experiment in the use of the Danish mouth-hand system, or a comparable method, in teaching young children. (An example of what appears to be a similar system has recently been devised at Gallaudet College, Washington, D.C. and is described in American Annals of the Deaf[1]). If such an experiment appeared to be feasible, a group of children taught in this way could be compared with a group taught by the Russian method and with a control group taught by purely oral methods.

An evaluation of the effects of combined media of communication (other than 311 to 313) when used at various stages of education

314. It was demonstrated by our enquiry into current practice (Chapter VI) that there are schools for the deaf in this country which make some use of manual media of communication in teaching. It is probable therefore that conditions exist which would make possible, without major innovation, an evaluation of the effects on the progress of children of different ages and types of various methods of combining finger spelling or signing or both with oral media. We hope that schools (which were not of course identified in our enquiry) will be prepared to offer to take part in controlled experiments in which groups of children are matched with comparable children whose education has been and is continuing by purely oral methods. We recommend the Department of Education and Science to invite all special schools for the deaf and the deaf and partially hearing to say, in due course, whether they would be prepared to take part in such experiments either as 'control' schools or 'experimental' schools. We recognise that effective research may be possible only if schools using combined media are willing to make some modifications in their practice, if these are necessary for experimental purposes, and perhaps, in some cases, to adopt a more co-ordinated approach within the school to media of communication, limiting the use of combined media to teachers with sufficient skill. We hope

that schools will be ready to co-operate in these ways in the interests of properly controlled research.

315. The purpose of these studies would be to evaluate the effects over a period of years of using various types of combined media and would preferably be carried out in two separate projects, one relating to pupils in the later stages of primary education and the other to secondary education. Each study would need to assess the effect which the introduction of combined media at various earlier stages of their education had produced in the pupils concerned.

Lipreading: factors of its effectiveness in communication

316. Research is needed into factors affecting the development of lipreading ability, including factors involved in the giving of accurate communication (lipreadability). This has important implications both for the initial and further training of teachers of the deaf and also, possibly, for their deployment within schools, where the ability to be lipread may be more important in some stages and aspects of education than in others.

Finger spelling: one handed and two handed spelling compared

317. A study is needed to compare the effectiveness of one-handed and two-handed finger spelling, if used in the education of children. It is clear that the former has an advantage in leaving one hand free and it seems likely that there is greater ease in watching hand and lip movements made simultaneously because the hand of the speaker can be held close to the mouth. Against these, there are the possible disadvantages that one-handed finger spelling may call for greater dexterity than some children possess and that it appears to be rather less expressive, purely as a form of manual gesturing, than the two-handed variety.

Finger spelling and speech: in practice, how far are they synchronised?

318. A number of the studies we have suggested will need to include investigations of the problems of synchronising oral and manual media. In paragraph 75, we drew particular attention to the difficulties which may occur in the use of residual hearing if the attempt to synchronise finger spelling with speech imposes an unnaturally slow pace and artificial rhythm on the spoken word, or, alternatively, if a normal tempo of speech is maintained but finger spelling is not synchronised. Pending the outcome of major studies, useful results might be obtained from a limited experiment with a small number of young deaf adults whose normal method of comprehending speech is by lip reading, supplemented by residual hearing, and who are familiar with the manual alphabet.

Signs: investigation into the possible uses of the new Paget system

319. The current use of the new Paget systematic sign language in a few schools seems likely to lead to further experiments by individual schools and teachers. In our view, it is desirable to mount a controlled experiment with somewhat larger groups of children than is possible within a single school. Accordingly we suggest that schools making use of the Paget system should be invited in due course to inform the Department of Education and Science so that consideration can be given to the establishment of such an experiment.

Part Three

The immediate situation and its problems

320. In our survey we have found unanimous agreement that measures could be taken to bring the linguistic development and educational achievement of deaf children to levels more compatible than at present with their potentialities. We have also been made aware of the many problems that must arise in any attempts to ameliorate the present situation.

321. With these views we are fully in accord; and in the recommendations that follow we draw attention to their practical implications. We have made clear our view that at present there are factors working against a successful use of purely oral methods in the education of some deaf children. Some of these factors may not be changed for some time to come. In recognition of this we have recommended research studies into methods of oral education and into the possibilities of supplementing oral education by the use of manual media of communication. But research studies require careful planning and evaluation; and operational research must extend over many years if it is to produce conclusive results. In the meantime schools for the deaf will be faced with the same difficult problems and decisions which now confront them and it is possible that some will wish to experiment more widely with teaching methods, including the use of combined media of communication for some children. Accordingly, we strongly recommend that their attention should be drawn to the desirability of observing certain general and more detailed pre-conditions which we propose to enumerate. Action will be required in some of these matters which is beyond the scope of the schools. In the paragraphs which follow we shall also draw the attention of all concerned to the conditions which we believe to be necessary for the promotion of oral education.

(i) General

Empirical approaches to media of communication, whether oral or manual, are unlikely to be helpful if the experimental methods cease to be used after a short period of time as children pass from the care of a single class teacher chosen for the work. Nor is much progress likely if there is no co-ordination of work in the experimental stages with that undertaken by the children before or after. Experiments carried out in the face of sustained opposition or hostility have little chance of producing satisfactory results. Local education authorities, voluntary bodies and heads could do much to create the right conditions by explaining to parents what is proposed, the reasons and the aims. Any such experiments must of course be distinguished from controlled investigations leading to answers of general application. We wish to make it quite clear that we do not regard such experiments as an adequate substitute for controlled research studies of the kind we have listed. Their purpose would be simply to produce better results in particular circumstances.

(ii) Oral education

We strongly recommend that every attempt should be made to give every deaf child the fullest opportunities of oral education, as defined in paragraphs 26 to 28.

We recommend therefore that without delay steps should be taken by all concerned to secure the conditions favourable to the oral education of deaf children, as set out in paragraphs 289 to 292. That is to say, action should be specially directed to:

(a) the establishment of comprehensive services in every area for the early detection of hearing impairment and other disabilities which may affect learning and for the expert guidance of parents:

(b) the promotion of good language teaching in schools for the deaf; and

(c) the extension of opportunities for the further education of young deaf people;

and to further these ends:

(d) a sufficient number of suitably qualified teachers of the deaf should be trained, and practising teachers should be encouraged and helped to take advantage of courses of further training; and

(e) in post-graduate medical education, and in the professional training or further training of psychologists, the need should be recognised for an increase in the number of special diagnostic teams, including psychiatrists, neurologists and psychologists who are informed and experienced in the problems of hearing and communication disorders in children.

(iii) **The selection and training of teachers for experimental work**

If a school decides to experiment with the use of combined media of communication for some of its pupils, it is of the greatest importance that it should be able to select teachers for this work who are skilled in the use of the chosen medium. No formal arrangements exist by which teachers can be trained in the use of manual media. We recommend therefore that those concerned with the professional education of teachers should consider what steps they can take, if necessary in co-operation with other agencies, to arrange suitable courses of training. We suggest that teachers should be given the opportunity of gaining the necessary expertise and studying its applications in the teaching of children by means of part-time courses, possibly supplemented by a short period of full-time training.

(iv) **Finger spelling**

(a) The Russian method of teaching young deaf children is complex and has many interdependent features. It may not be capable of transplantation without modification and we would not recommend its ad hoc adoption in this country. We have recommended a detailed preliminary study leading to a controlled experiment. Pending the outcome of this, and bearing in mind that most of our evidence was opposed to the use of finger spelling at an early stage, we suggest that it is generally inadvisable to use finger spelling in teaching children up to the stage of about six years.

(b) We recommend that teachers of older children who make occasional use of letters of the manual alphabet to indicate phonemes which are difficult or impossible to lipread should make themselves familiar with the work done in Denmark and with the phonetic basis of English speech sounds.

(c) We recommend that careful attention should be given to the possibility that any method which seeks to combine finger spelling continuously and simultaneously with speech may create problems of distraction or synchronisation (paragraph 75).

(d) We recommend that care is taken by any school which decides to use finger spelling to ensure that the speed of execution is compatible with the children's ability to comprehend what is being presented.

(e) Finger spelling might be justified for pupils with a basic oral proficiency for whom it was proposed as a means of accelerating the speed of imparting information. This use of finger spelling was suggested by many witnesses.

(f) The use of finger spelling as a supplement to oral media, reading and writing was suggested by a number of witnesses as a means of helping deaf pupils with poor lipreading ability for which their residual hearing compensates inadequately. For children who seem to be intellectually retarded or to suffer from speech and language disorders, schools which are inclined to experiment with finger spelling are recommended to watch with great care whether this is, in fact, conducive to progress.

(g) In considering the above recommendations about the use of finger spelling, it should be borne in mind that some people take the view that its use is incompatible with the aim of integration in hearing society.

(v) Signing

(a) It was argued by some witnesses that the unsystematic character and lack of grammatical structure in conventional signing need not be a barrier to the use of individual signs as part of a combined medium consisting also of speech and finger spelling. If teachers use signs in this way, we recommend that they should control and select them with care, avoiding unsuitable usages.

(b) It was also brought to our notice that signing might tend to become the dominant element, if not in class then in communication among children, and might interfere with oral progress and linguistic development. We believe that there are such risks, but this can only be determined by detailed investigation over a long period. If schools decide to accept such risks, we recommend that they should seek to minimise them by combining signs with other media in normal language patterns and by ensuring that the sequence is that of the mother tongue.

(c) Clearly the major risks associated with the use of a combined method which includes signing would be eliminated if the signs used were themselves chosen from a systematic language with normal grammatical structure. We have already said that in our view the new Paget sign language is such a system and we have noted with great interest the experimental work which is going on in some schools. Among our proposed research projects we have recommended the establishment of a controlled experiment in the use of the Paget system as an educational medium.

(d) We have referred in paragraph 309 to the desirability of making special provision, if only by separate teaching arrangements within schools, for those children with additional or special disabilities who have the most severe communication difficulties. We have recommended that systematic experimental work involving interdisciplinary teams should be undertaken in a few schools. Every special school providing classes for such children should however, in our view, feel free to make whatever use of signs, natural gestures and mime they consider necessary to establish communication in some form and from this to lead on to such educational and social progress as may be possible. We believe that the aim with these children, as with others, should be to develop normal patterns of language even if in simple forms.

The balance between elements in a combined medium of communication

322. In offering this guidance, we have been concerned with methods of combining various kinds of manual media with oral media; but we have not found it possible to suggest specific balances between them, or between finger spelling and signing within a combined oral-manual method, which could be considered appropriate to serve one or other of a number of specific purposes. As Chapter X demonstrates, many nice distinctions can be made and are deserving of study; but precise recommendations cannot be made at this stage in the absence of evidence from research.

The stage of introduction

323. If finger spelling or signing is introduced in the education of deaf children the stage of introduction must depend upon the purpose intended to be served i.e. to assist the establishment of oral communication, to provide a substitute for it, to supplement it, or simply to provide school leavers with a ready means of communication with other deaf people in adult life. In the case of the second and third of these alternatives, fine judgments are involved as to the point at which substitution or supplementation appears to be necessary, taking into account a variety of factors affecting individual children. Schools which decide to experiment with these methods cannot assume therefore that either a particular age or a particular stage of education is likely to be the most generally suitable. We have, however, indicated in paragraph 321(iv) (a) that pending the outcome of controlled experiments, finger spelling with very young children should be used with great caution, if used at all.

The organization of education for children taught by different media of communication

324. Although there is a view that separation is undesirable, experienced practitioners and observers have concluded that deaf children who are potentially capable of making progress in speech and language by purely oral methods will not make adequate progress if they associate with children who are being taught by finger spelling or signing in addition to oral media. They advocate the complete separation of the two groups. Our own view is that a general application of the principle of complete separation would not be justified in advance of a long term investigation on a wider scale than has been possible hitherto, although we accept that there are special considerations in the case of children with the most severe communication difficulties (paragraph 309) and that similar considerations might apply to other children for whom the manual element might predominate in a combined mode of communication (but see paragraph 327). We must point out, however, the organisational and other problems which might be involved both in the short term and the long term if a policy of separation were seen as always involving the provision of completely separate schools.

325. In the immediate future no general reorganisation of schools for the deaf to implement such a policy would be practicable since there is no factual evidence of the number and types of children likely to be found in the various groups. We have expressed the belief that measures will be taken which will increase the numbers of children able to benefit from purely oral methods of education and for the purpose of argument we will postulate that in the long term there will be only a minority of deaf pupils taught through combined media. If the children were separated, there would either have to be small departments of existing schools or separate schools of a sufficient size to be viable in terms of staffing and organisation. The adoption of the second alternative would mean the provision of a handful of schools specialising in the use of combined media to serve the whole country and would inevitably require some children who at present attend day schools to become boarding pupils. For many boarders at these schools the possibilities of home visits during term-time would be extremely limited in view of the large areas of the country which each school would serve.

326. It seems to us therefore that, in the short term, to ensure that adequate progress of pupils by purely oral methods is not adversely affected, organisational measures *within* schools might be advisable to promote the educational progress of those children who seem to need some supplementation of oral by manual media. These measures might also prove to be the optimal solution in the long term for this group of children.

327. There are children for whom the manual element may predominate. These include some with special or additional disabilities, on the organisation of whose education we find ourselves in general agreement (paragraphs 309, 321 (v) (d) and 324). But in respect of other children for whom the manual element may predominate, there are differences of view among us which reflect personal experience and take into account in different ways the opinions brought in evidence to us. Some of us believe that it would be desirable for the education of these children to be organised within the same schools as that of children for whom the manual element is subsidiary or entirely absent; others take the view that it would be to their benefit and to that of other children if separate departments or separate schools were provided.

Part Four

Summary of Recommendations

1. The aim of educating children with impaired hearing should be to enable them to realise their full potential and as far as possible take their place in society as literate adults with whole personalities which they can express through generally understood media of communication (Paragraph 282).

2. Partially hearing pupils should be excluded from the scope of research or experimentation with manual media of communication. This exclusion should not necessarily apply to young children with severe hearing losses whose ultimate educational classification is uncertain (Paragraphs 283 and 284).

3. Conditions should be established as soon as possible which are favourable to the oral education of deaf children (Paragraphs 289–292; see also 9 below).

4. Research studies should be undertaken to determine whether or not and in what circumstances the introduction of manual media of communication would lead to improvement in the education of deaf children (Paragraph 294).

5. There should be established an informal consultative body to advise the Department of Education and Science on the design of research proposals, on the initiation of discussions with research bodies, and on the dissemination of research results (Paragraph 295). The inception of a research programme should not, however, wait upon the establishment of this consultative machinery (Paragraph 297).

6. The Schools Council for the Curriculum and Examinations should be invited to consider the need for promoting and supporting research and development in the education of deaf children (Paragraph 296).

7. Local education authorities and the managers of non-maintained schools for children with impaired hearing should consider to what extent existing forms of record and sources of information relating to individual pupils are adequate and should notify the Department of Education and Science of any major inadequacies. The Department should consult with these bodies on the adoption of appropriate and adequate school records (Paragraph 298).

8. Research and investigation should concentrate upon:
   (a) detailed investigation of practice in schools (Paragraphs 300 and 301);
   (b) devising measures of linguistic attainment (Paragraph 302);
   (c) studies of individual children (Paragraphs 303–310);
   (d) effects of combining oral and manual media (Paragraphs 311–315);
   (e) processes in oral and manual communication (Paragraphs 316–319).

9. All concerned should take the steps indicated to secure the conditions in which every deaf child can have the fullest opportunities of oral education (Paragraph 321 (ii)).

10. Schools which decide to experiment with the use of combined media of communication for some children pending the outcome of research, should observe certain general and more detailed considerations which are enumerated. In some of these considerations they will require help from those concerned with the professional education of teachers of the deaf and from local education authorities and voluntary bodies which maintain special schools for children with impaired hearing (Paragraph 321 (i), (iii), (iv) and (v)).

11. In the absence of evidence from research, no general guidance can be given on a suitable balance between elements in a combined medium of communication (Paragraph 322).

12. Similarly, no general guidance can be given on the stage at which finger-spelling or signing might be introduced (Paragraph 323).

13. Organisational measures within schools may be advisable to meet the needs of those children who seem to need some supplementation of oral by manual media side by side with those children making adequate progress by purely oral methods (Paragraphs 324 to 326).

14. With regard to the organisation of the education of those children for whom manual media may predominate (other than children with additional or

special disabilities), there are differences of view among us and we can only recommend that consideration be given to these different views (Paragraph 327).

REFERENCE

1. Cornett, R. Orin 'Cued Speech' American Annals of the Deaf, January, 1967, 112, 1, 3–13.

(*Signed*)   M. M. LEWIS (*Chairman*)
R. MONICA CLARE
JOHN C. DENMARK
JOHN J. KELLY
PETER GASKILL
SYLVIA M. GRAY
R. GULLIFORD
T. S. LITTLER
K. P. MURPHY
NORAH L. NORTH
MICHAEL REED
GEO. E. ROBINSON
E. M. SHEAVYN
H. H. SHORROCK
IAN G. TAYLOR
M. D. VERNON

J. M. SCRIMSHAW
(*Secretary*)

B. P. LINCOLN
(*Assistant Secretary*)

Note of Reservation on School Experimentation
by Mr. P. Gaskill and Professor I. G. Taylor
(Chapter XIII, Part Three)

With regard to experimentation in schools, in our view no precautions, even of the kind suggested in Part three of Chapter XIII, however carefully observed, are an adequate substitute for properly controlled research studies. Pending the outcome of these, experimentation with manual media of communication in schools for the deaf should, in our view, be discouraged.

We also believe that too much attention has been focussed on possible palliatives at the expense of the central issues—the urgent need for more teachers of the deaf and for adequate facilities for diagnosis, assessment and parent guidance.

We feel strongly that until we are able to make more precise diagnoses about individual children's learning problems, we are not in a position to advise about possible changes in the present methods of educating deaf children.

A Note by The Chairman

In view of the statement made in the first sentence of the note of reservation by Professor Taylor and Mr. Gaskill, I have been asked by the rest of the Committee to draw attention to paragraph 321 of our report, in which we make clear that we do not regard school experimentation of the kind discussed in Part three of Chapter XIII as an adequate substitute for controlled research.

M. M. Lewis

List of Witnesses

The symbol † denotes that both oral and written evidence was given; witnesses who gave oral evidence only are shown by an asterisk. All other witnesses submitted written evidence only.

(i) Organisations

British Association of the Hard of Hearing
British Deaf and Dumb Association
Church of England Council for the Deaf
National College of Teachers of the Deaf
National Deaf Children's Society
National Council of Missioners and Welfare Officers to the Deaf (†Oral evidence for the Council was given by Alderman R. Stavers Oloman and the Rev. G. C. Firth)
Royal Association in Aid of the Deaf and Dumb
Royal National Institute for the Deaf
Scottish Association for the Deaf

(ii) Teachers

Mr. J. Baden Powell, Headmaster, Llandrindod Wells School (now retired)
† Mr. S. J. Blount, Headmaster, Nutfield Priory School, Redhill
Dr. D. M. C. Dale, Headmaster, The School for the Deaf, Kelston, Auckland, New Zealand (Dr. Dale later gave evidence in his capacity of Senior Lecturer in the Education of the Deaf, University of London Institute of Education)
Mr. G. H. Dalziel, Headmaster, Hartley House School, Plymouth
† Mr. F. G. W. Denmark, Headmaster, Jordanstown School, Northern Ireland
Mr. F. W. Flaherty, Headmaster, Moor House School, Oxted, Surrey
Mr. H. J. S. Furness, Headmaster, The School for the Partially Hearing, Birkdale, Southport
Miss W. Galbraith, Audiology Unit, Royal Ear Hospital, Huntley Street, London, W.C.1
† Dr. E. S. Greenaway, retired; formerly headmaster of the Yorkshire Residential School for the Deaf, Doncaster
Miss P. M. Griffiths, Royal School for Deaf Children, Birmingham
† Mr. F. W. Hockenhull, Headmaster, Northern Counties School for the Deaf (now headmaster of the Yorkshire Residential School for the Deaf, Doncaster)
† Mr. W. Jeffrey, Headmaster, Donaldson's School, Edinburgh
Miss J. Kerr Cross, formerly at the City Literary Institute, London
* Mrs. A. McMillan, Glasgow School for the Deaf
† Mother Mary Nicholas, Headmistress, St. Mary's School, Cabra, Dublin
Miss M. Palmer, Headmistress, John Horniman School, Worthing
Mrs. J. Pendlebury, Manchester Hearing Aid Clinic
Mr. T. Pursglove, Headmaster, Royal School for Deaf Children, Margate
Mr. J. D. Pym, formerly teacher of the deaf in schools in England, Canada and the U.S.A.
Miss J. E. Shields, Pathways Unit, Condover Hall School, Shrewsbury
† Mr. A. E. Steel, Bridge House School, Harewood, Yorkshire
Miss A. Stonehold, now at Larchmoor School
Brother P. J. Walsh, St. Joseph's School, Cabra, Dublin
Mr. H. G. Williams, now a member of H.M. Inspectorate of Schools
Mrs. P. Wolfe, Stoneleigh School, Leicester
† Mr. W. E. Wood, Burwood Park School, Walton on Thames, Surrey
Miss D. E. Woodford, Royal School for Deaf Children, Margate

(iii) University of London Institute of Education

Dr. D. M. C. Dale (see also under (ii))

(iv) **University of Manchester Department of Audiology and Education of the Deaf**

    Mr. G. B. Campbell
    Miss E. H. Carhill
* Emeritus Professor Sir Alexander Ewing
    Mrs. N. H. Moseley
    Miss J. Palmer
† Dr. T. J. Watson
    Miss M. B. Williamson
    Dr. D. C. Wollman (now a member of H.M. Inspectorate of Schools)

(v) **Inspectors and former inspectors of schools**

* Mr. J. H. Blount, formerly Inspector of Special Education with the London County Council (Headmaster of Rayners School, Penn, at the time of giving evidence)
    Mr. H. E. Chalkley, H.M.I. (Ministry of Education, Northern Ireland)
† Mr. L. C. Holroyde, formerly Special Schools Adviser with the Liverpool local education authority
† Miss E. M. Johnson, H.M.I.
† Mr. J. Lumsden, H.M.I. (retired)
† Mr. A. T. Parnham, H.M.I. (retired)
† Mr. D. S. Petrie, H.M.I. (Scottish Education Department)
† Mr. W. H. Snowdon, H.M.I.

In addition, we asked one of our members, Mr. M. M. Reed, Inspector of Special Education with the Inner London Education Authority, to prepare a memorandum for us.

(vi) **Medical witnesses and other witnesses invited to give evidence from research or clinical experience**

    Professor D. Abercrombie, Head of the Phonetics Department, University of Edinburgh
    Mr. J. C. Ballantyne, Consultant Otologist, The Royal Free Hospital, Grays Inn Road, London, W.C.1.
    Miss A. H. Bowley, Educational Psychologist, Children's Unit, Belmont Hospital, Sutton, Surrey
    Mrs. F. Cavanagh, Aural Surgeon, Royal Manchester Children's Hospital
    Air Vice Marshall E. D. D. Dickson, Chairman, Royal National Institute for the Deaf
    Dr. R. W. Eldridge, formerly Principal Senior Medical Officer, Lancashire County Council
    Professor D. B. Fry, Professor of Experimental Phonetics, University College, London
    Mr. A. P. Fuller, Ear, Nose and Throat Surgeon, St. Bartholomew's Hospital, London, E.C.1.
† Dr. P. Henderson, Principal Medical Officer, Department of Education and Science
    Mr. R. Hunt Williams, Director, Audiology Research Unit, Royal Berkshire Hospital, Reading
† Dr. C. B. Huss, Senior Medical Officer, Department of Education and Science
    Mr. G. Livingstone, Consultant Otologist, Department of Otolaryngology, The Radcliffe Infirmary, Oxford
    Mrs. M. J. Malloy, Teacher, Children's Unit, Belmont Hospital, Sutton, Surrey
    Dr. L. Minski, Physician in Charge, Children's Unit, Belmont Hospital, Sutton, Surrey
    Mr. J. I. Munro Black, Consultant Otologist, Royal Victoria Infirmary, Newcastle-upon-Tyne 1
    Mr. J. H. Otty, Consultant Otologist, Ear, Nose, Throat and Eye Unit, Bradford Royal Infirmary
† Dr. E. E. Simpson, Senior Medical Officer, Department of Education and Science
    Mr. I. S. Thompson, Ear, Nose and Throat Surgeon, Aberdeen Royal Infirmary
    Dr. S. Yudkin, Paediatrician, Whittington Hospital, Highgate Wing, London N.19

In addition, we asked one of our members, Dr. J. C. Denmark, Consultant Psychiatrist, Manchester Regional Hospital Board, to prepare a memorandum for us.

(vii) Individuals concerned in the welfare of deaf adolescents and adults

Mr. W. Archer, Missioner and Welfare Officer, Blake Lodge Centre for the Deaf, Plymouth

Miss E. Arthur, retired, formerly teacher of the deaf

Miss D. K. Barker, Welfare Officer to the Deaf, St. Albans Diocesan Association for the Deaf and/or Dumb

Rev. S. Barnett, Chaplain, Royal Association in Aid of the Deaf and Dumb

Rev. B. T. Bean, Chaplain Superintendent, Sussex Diocesan Association for the Deaf and Dumb

Miss B. M. Bevan, trainee Welfare Officer, Oxford Diocesan Council for the Deaf

Mr. F. Bradley, Superintendent, R.N.I.D. Home, Poolemead, Twerton-on-Avon, Bath

Miss C. Brooke-Hughes, Welfare Officer for the Deaf, Ministry of Health

Mr. G. D. Campbell, Hon. Secretary and Treasurer, Scottish Regional Council, British Deaf and Dumb Association

Mr. R. C. Coles, Royal National Institute for the Deaf, Editor of 'Hearing'

Mr. E. R. Collins, Vice-President, British Deaf and Dumb Association

Rev. P. T. Corfmat, Chaplain and Welfare Officer, Canterbury Diocesan Association for the Deaf

Mr. P. J. Dalladay, Social Welfare Officer for the Deaf, Glamorgan County Council

Mr. A. F. Dimmock, Hon. Secretary, St. Francis Social and Sports Club for the Deaf, Redhill, Surrey, and Organising Secretary, British Deaf Tourists Movement

Mr. R. Drewry, Research Student, now Town and Country Planning Assistant (see also under (ix))

Mr. E. Dujardin, Superintendent, Ernest Ayliffe Home for the Aged and Infirm Deaf and Dumb, Rawton, Leeds

Rev. K. Earle, Chaplain-Secretary, Northamptonshire and Rutland Mission to the Deaf

Mr. G. T. M. English, Missioner and Welfare Officer, Buckinghamshire Centre Committee, Oxford Diocesan Council for the Deaf

Mr. T. J. Evans, formerly Missioner, Chester and North Wales Deaf and Dumb Society

Mr. H. Feeney, Superintendent Missioner, Glamorgan and Monmouthshire Missions to the Adult Deaf and Dumb

† Rev. G. C. Firth, Hon. Secretary, West Regional Association for the Deaf

Rev. R. B. S. Gillman, Chairman, Oxford Diocesan Council for the Deaf

Rev. F. Goodridge, Bishop's Chaplain to the Deaf, Oxford Diocesan Council for the Deaf

Mr. C. G. Griffiths, Missioner, Church Mission to the Deaf and Dumb in Walsall, Wednesbury and Mid. Staffordshire

Rev. N. M. Harrison, Chaplain to the Deaf, Diocese of Sheffield

Mr. W. F. Kelly, Missioner, Church Mission to the Deaf and Dumb, South Staffordshire and Shropshire

Mr. J. M. E. King, Hon. Secretary, North East Children's Association

Miss M. Little, Welfare Officer, Salisbury Diocesan Association for the Deaf and Hard of Hearing

Rev. J. S. Lochrie, Minister and Secretary, Glasgow and West of Scotland Mission to the Deaf and Dumb

Rev. A. F. Mackenzie, Chaplain-Secretary. Salisbury Diocesan Association for the Deaf and Hard of Hearing

Miss J. E. Mac Innes, County Council Representative, Carlisle Diocesan Association for the Deaf

Miss A. M. Martin, Matron, St. John's Home, Oxford

Mr. M. B. Mason, Hon. Secretary and Treasurer. The London Deaf Club

Rev. B. B. Morgan, formerly Chaplain, Royal Association in Aid of the Deaf and Dumb

Rev. D. O'Farrell, Chaplain and Organiser, St. Vincent's After-Care Society for the Deaf, Glasgow N.W.

* Lady Grace Paget

Mr. A. Ross, Superintendent, Gloucester Diocesan Association for the Deaf

† Mr. K. Scarratt, Welfare Officer to the Deaf, Stoke on Trent Institute for the Deaf

Mr. M. C. A. Smith, Superintendent, Oldham Society for the Deaf

111

Mr. M. G. Speed, County Welfare Officer, Devon County Council
Mr. A. Stephenson, Superintendent, South Durham and North Yorkshire Association for the Deaf
† Rev. Canon T. H. Sutcliffe, Secretary, Church of England Council for the Deaf
Rev. J. N. Veysey, Chaplain and Welfare Officer, Somerset Diocesan Mission to the Deaf
The Very Rev. I. H. White Thompson, Chairman, Church of England Council for the Deaf

In addition, we asked one of our members, Mrs. E. M. Sheavyn, formerly Further Education and Youth Officer of the British Deaf and Dumb Association to prepare a memorandum for us.

(viii) Youth Employment Officers concerned with the placement of handicapped school leavers
Mrs. M. C. Clarke
Miss B. Leicester
Mr. E. Mitchell
Mr. C. Webber

(ix) Deaf witnesses
Mrs. H. Beaumont
Mrs. H. M. Beckett
Mr. M. Bladon
Mrs. W. A. Brand
Mr. D. A. Brown
Mrs. M. E. Cleary
Miss C. Cooney
* Mrs. V. Danzig
Mr. G. Donaldson
Mr. R. Drewry (see also under (vii))
Mr. R. Fell
Mr. D. Fyfe
Mr. T. L. Gardner
* Dr. Pierre Gorman
Mr. B. J. Harmsworth
Mr. D. T. Harris
Mr. W. Jackson
Miss D. Johnson
Mr. T. A. Lawrence
Mr. W. Lettress
† Mr. C. Marsh
Mrs. E. J. Marson
Miss D. S. Miles
Miss D. Moore
Mrs. G. Morgan
* Mrs. M. Oliver
Mr. A. Reeves
Mrs. A. Rothwell
Mr. H. Rowe
Mr. M. Sabell
Mr. T. Shaw
Miss I. G. M. Smith
Mrs. W. L. Stanford
* Mr. M. Surey
Mrs. E. Squire
Mr. & Mrs. J. Syrett
Mr. T. L. Waters.

Other deaf people were interviewed as part of the survey referred to in Chapter XI, or wrote to us through their Welfare Officers.

(x) Other individual witnesses, including parents of deaf children

Mrs. M. Bentley
Mr. P. Denton
Mrs. E. E. Dodd
Mr. & Mrs. H. K. Drewett
Mr. P. Goodridge
Mrs. J. Green
Mr. G. M. Hull
Mr. J. G. Hull
Mr. & Mrs. M. Kennedy
Mrs. C. Macdonald
Mr. A. Morgan
Mr. J. M. Paul
Miss L. Pemberton
Miss S. Quick
Mrs. M. P. Reynish
Mr. F. P. Robins
Dr. F. Sandy
Mrs. M. Shaw
Mr. P. D. Taylor

(xi) Visitors from the U.S.A. who addressed the Committee

Dr. Powrie Vaux Doctor, Editor, American Annals of the Deaf
Professor Hans Furth, The Catholic University of America
Professor Stephen P. Quigley, Professor of Special Education, University of Illinois Institute for Research on Exceptional Children

(xii) Other evidence

Dr. P. Henderson and Mr. R. Howlett of the Department of Education and Science prepared a report for us on their visit to the U.S.S.R. to study Russian methods of teaching young deaf children.

Media of communication used in the education of
children with impaired hearing in Great Britain

An enquiry by questionnaire
(See Chapter VI, paragraphs 109 to 111)

On the following page is reproduced the questionnaire which was addressed to all special schools and independent schools for pupils with impaired hearing and all special classes for partially hearing pupils at ordinary schools in England, Wales and Scotland.

The tables on the pages following the questionnaire summarise the replies received.

Please place √ in the appropriate space	
Boarding school for deaf	
Day school for Deaf	
Boarding school for deaf and partially hearing	
Day school for Deaf and partially hearing	
Boarding school for partially hearing	
Special class or unit for partially hearing	

Please complete a separate form for each stage and insert number on roll (for the stage in question only) in the appropriate space.	Number on Roll
Nursery and Infant stage	
Junior stage	
Secondary stage	

		By children to children			By children to teachers			By teachers to children			Between child care staff and children		
		never	sometimes	often	never	sometimes	often	never	sometimes	often	never	sometimes	often
*Is natural gesture ever used in your school?	in class												
	out of class												
†Are 'signs' ever used in your school?	in class												
	out of class												
Is finger spelling ever used in your school?	in class												
	out of class												

Please place √ in the appropriate spaces.
* By natural gesture we mean the kind of mime or gesture used widely in normal nursery and infant school story telling or when in a foreign country if the language is not known.
† By 'signs' we mean any arbitrary movement of hands excluding finger spelling and mime.
Please add any explanatory comments if necessary.
If any of these methods are used with some special categories, such as dull, C.P. or maladjusted children, or children of deaf parents, would you indicate below.

No. and type of schools where finger spelling is used by teachers to children

England and Wales

Type of School	Stage	Total No. of returns		Sometimes	Often	Percentages of returns Sometimes	Often
Boarding Schools for the deaf.	Nursery and infant	12	In Class	2	—	16·6	—
			Out of Class	2	—	16·6	—
	Junior	13	In Class	5	—	38·4	—
			Out of Class	5	—	38·4	—
	Secondary	13	In Class	5	2	38·4	15·4
			Out of Class	4	3	30·7	23·0
Boarding Schools for the deaf and partially hearing.	Nursery and infant	8	In Class	—	—	—	—
			Out of Class	—	—	—	—
	Junior	10	In Class	5	—	50·0	—
			Out of Class	6	—	60·0	—
	Secondary	8	In Class	2	3	25·0	37·5
			Out of Class	3	2	37·5	25·0
Boarding Schools for the partially hearing.	Nursery and infant	4	In Class	—	—	—	—
			Out of Class	—	—	—	—
	Junior	5	In Class	—	—	—	—
			Out of Class	—	—	—	—
	Secondary	5	In Class	—	—	—	—
			Out of Class	—	—	—	—
Day Schools for the deaf.	Nursery and infant	9	In Class	1	—	11·1	—
			Out of Class	1	—	11·1	—
	Junior	9	In Class	3	—	33·3	—
			Out of Class	1	—	11·1	—
	Secondary	6	In Class	4	—	66·6	—
			Out of Class	4	—	66·6	—
Day Schools for deaf and partially hearing.	Nursery and infant	10	In Class	1	—	10·0	—
			Out of Class	1	—	10·0	—
	Junior	10	In Class	2	—	20·0	—
			Out of Class	2	—	20·0	—
	Secondary	10	In Class	4	—	40·0	—
			Out of Class	5	—	50·0	—
Partially Hearing Units.	Nursery and infant	43	In Class	—	—	—	—
			Out of Class	—	—	—	—
	Junior	62	In Class	1	—	1·6	—
			Out of Class	1	—	1·6	—
	Secondary	20	In Class	1	—	5·0	—
			Out of Class	1	—	5·0	—

No. and type of schools where signs are used
by teachers to children

England and Wales

Type of School	Stage	Total No. of returns		Sometimes	Often	Percentages of returns Sometimes	Often
Boarding Schools for the deaf.	Nursery and infant	12	In Class	3	—	25·0	—
			Out of Class	3	—	25·0	—
	Junior	13	In Class	3	—	23·0	—
			Out of Class	3	—	23·0	—
	Secondary	13	In Class	8	—	61·5	—
			Out of Class	8	—	61·5	—
Boarding Schools for the deaf and partially hearing.	Nursery and infant	8	In Class	1	—	12·5	—
			Out of Class	1	—	12·5	—
	Junior	10	In Class	3	1	30·0	10·0
			Out of Class	3	1	30·0	10·0
	Secondary	8	In Class	2	1	25·0	12·5
			Out of Class	2	1	25·0	12·5
Boarding Schools for the partially hearing.	Nursery and infant	4	In Class	—	—	—	—
			Out of Class	—	—	—	—
	Junior	5	In Class	—	—	—	—
			Out of Class	—	—	—	—
	Secondary	5	In Class	—	—	—	—
			Out of Class	—	—	—	—
Day Schools for the deaf.	Nursery and infant	9	In Class	2	—	22·2	—
			Out of Class	2	—	22·2	—
	Junior	9	In Class	1	—	11·1	—
			Out of Class	1	—	11·1	—
	Secondary	6	In Class	2	—	33·3	—
			Out of Class	2	—	33·3	—
Day Schools for the deaf and partially hearing.	Nursery and infant	10	In Class	1	—	10·0	—
			Out of Class	1	—	10·0	—
	Junior	10	In Class	—	—	—	—
			Out of Class	—	—	—	—
	Secondary	10	In Class	—	—	—	—
			Out of Class	—	—	—	—
Partially Hearing Units.	Nursery and infant	43	In Class	1	—	2·3	—
			Out of Class	—	—	—	—
	Junior	62	In Class	1	—	1·6	—
			Out of Class	3	—	4·8	—
	Secondary	20	In Class	2	—	10·0	—
			Out of Class	2	—	10·0	—

No. and type of schools where signs and finger spelling are used by teachers to children

Scotland

Type of School Signs	Stage	Total No. of returns		Sometimes	Often	Percentages of returns Sometimes	Often
Boarding Schools for the deaf and partially hearing.	Nursery and infant	4	In Class	—	—	—	—
			Out of Class	—	—	—	—
	Junior	4	In Class	2	—	50·0	—
			Out of Class	2	—	50·0	—
	Secondary	4	In Class	2	—	50·0	—
			Out of Class	3	—	75·0	—
Day Schools for the deaf and partially hearing.	Nursery and infant	7	In Class	—	—	—	—
			Out of Class	—	—	—	—
	Junior	7	In Class	—	—	—	—
			Out of Class	—	—	—	—
	Secondary	7	In Class	—	1	—	14·3
			Out of Class	—	1	—	14·3
Partially Hearing Units.	Nursery and infant	1	In Class	1	—	100·0	—
			Out of Class	1	—	100·0	—
	Junior	1	In Class	1	—	100·0	—
			Out of Class	1	—	100·0	—
	Secondary	1	In Class	—	—	—	—
			Out of Class	1	—	100·0	—
Finger Spelling Boarding Schools for the deaf and partially hearing.	Nursery and infant	4	In Class	—	—	—	—
			Out of Class	—	—	—	—
	Junior	4	In Class	3	—	75·0	—
			Out of Class	4	—	100·0	—
	Secondary	4	In Class	4	—	100·0	—
			Out of Class	3	—	75·0	—
Day Schools for the deaf and partially hearing.	Nursery and infant	7	In Class	—	—	—	—
			Out of Class	—	—	—	—
	Junior	7	In Class	1	—	14·3	—
			Out of Class	—	—	—	—
	Secondary	7	In Class	—	—	—	—
			Out of Class	—	—	—	—
Partially Hearing Units.	Nursery and infant	1	In Class	—	—	—	—
			Out of Class	—	—	—	—
	Junior	1	In Class	—	—	—	—
			Out of Class	—	—	—	—
	Secondary	1	In Class	—	1	100·0	—
			Out of Class	—	1	100·0	—

Boarding Schools for the Deaf

Nursery and Infant Stage — 12 Returns including 1 with incomplete ticks

		Children to Children			Children to Teachers			Teachers to Children			Child Care Staff		
		N	S	O	N	S	O	N	S	O	N	S	O
Natural Gesture	in class	1	3	8	1	4	7	1	8	3	1	5	6
	out of class	1	3	8	1	4	7	1	8	3			
Signs	in class	7	4		7	4		8	3		7	4	
	out of class	6	5		7	4		8	3				
Finger Spelling	in class	9	2(a)		9	2(a)		9	2(a)		9	2(a)	
	out of class	9	2(a)		9	2(a)		9	2(a)				

(a) One of these entries in each case occurs in the return of a school which explains that there is so high a proportion of children with dual handicaps (e.g. deafness and educational subnormality) that it becomes essential to use non oral methods if these children are to be contacted at all.

Junior Stage — 13 Returns

		Children to Children			Children to Teachers			Teachers to Children			Child Care Staff		
		N	S	O	N	S	O	N	S	O	N	S	O
Natural Gesture	in class	1	4	8	1	7	5	1	10	2	1	8	4
	out of class	1	1	11	1	6	6	1	10	2			
Signs	in class	2	9	2	4	9			10	3	6	7	
	out of class	2	6	5	3	10			10	3			
Finger Spelling	in class	6	6	1	9	4		8	5		9	4	
	out of class	5	7	1	9	4		8	5				

Secondary Stage — 13 Returns including 2 with incomplete ticks

		Children to Children			Children to Teachers			Teachers to Children			Child Care Staff		
		N	S	O	N	S	O	N	S	O	N	S	O
Natural Gesture	in class	1	5	7	1	9	3	1	9	3	1	6	5
	out of class	1	3	9	1	9	3	1	9	3			
Signs	in class	3	6	4	6	6	1	5	8		5	5	3
	out of class	2	2	8	5	7	1	5	8				
Finger Spelling	in class	3	5	2	6	4	3	6	5	2	8	4	1
	out of class	4	6	3	5	5	3	6	4	3			

Boarding Schools for Deaf and Partially Hearing

Nursery and Infant Stage

8 returns including 1 with incomplete ticks

		Children to Children			Children to Teachers			Teachers to Children			Child Care Staff		
		N	S	O	N	S	O	N	S	O	N	S	O
Natural Gesture	in class		3	5		4	4	1(a)	5	2		5	3
	out of class		2	6		4	4	1(a)	5	2			
Signs	in class	4	3	1	4	4		7	1			4	4
	out of class	4	2	2	4	4		7	1				
Finger Spelling	in class	7	1		8			7				7	1
	out of class	7	1		7			7					

Junior Stage

10 Returns including 1 with incomplete ticks

		Children to Children			Children to Teachers			Teachers to Children			Child Care Staff		
		N	S	O	N	S	O	N	S	O	N	S	O
Natural Gesture	in class		4	6	1	3	6	1(a)	6	3	1(a)	6	2
	out of class		3	7	1	3	6	1(a)	4	5			
Signs	in class	2	6	2	2	6	1	6	3	1	4	4	1
	out of class	2	3	5	2	7	1	6	3	1			
Finger Spelling	in class	5	3	2	5	4	1	5	5		4	3	2
	out of class	5	4	1	5	5		4	6				

Secondary Stage

8 Returns

		Children to Children			Children to Teachers			Teachers to Children			Child Care Staff		
		N	S	O	N	S	O	N	S	O	N	S	O
Natural Gesture	in class		5	3		6	2		6	2	1	5	2
	out of class		4	4		6	2		6	2			
Signs	in class	2	4	2	3	3	2	5	2	1	4	4	
	out of class	1	3	4	3	3	2	5	2	1			
Finger Spelling	in class	3	3	2	3	4	1	4*	2	3*	4	2	2
	out of class	3	2	3	3	5		4*	3	2*			

*One School duplicated entries in the 'Never' and 'Often' columns as indicated. They explained that 'Never' applied to partially hearing pupils and 'Often' to deaf pupils.
(a) These entries all occur in the returns of one school.

Nursery and Infant Stage   4 Returns

		Children to Children			Children to Teachers			Teachers to Children			Child Care Staff		
		N	S	O	N	S	O	N	S	O	N	S	O
Natural Gesture	in class		2	2		3	1	1	2	1		2	2
	out of class		2	2		2	2	1	2	1			
Signs	in class	3	1		3	1		4			4		
	out of class	1	3		3	1		4					
Finger Spelling	in class	4			4			4			4		
	out of class	4			4			4					

Junior Stage   5 Returns

		Children to Children			Children to Teachers			Teachers to Children			Child Care Staff		
		N	S	O	N	S	O	N	S	O	N	S	O
Natural Gesture	in class	1	3	1		4	1	1	4			4	1
	out of class		4	1		4	1	1	4				
Signs	in class	4	1		4	1		5			4	1	
	out of class	3	2		4	1		5					
Finger Spelling	in class	5			5			5			4	1	
	out of class	5			5			5					

Secondary Stage   5 Returns

		Children to Children			Children to Teachers			Teachers to Children			Child Care Staff		
		N	S	O	N	S	O	N	S	O	N	S	O
Natural Gesture	in class	2	3			5		2	3		1	4	
	out of class	1	3	1		5		2	3				
Signs	in class	4	1		5			5			5		
	out of class	3	1	1	5			5					
Finger Spelling	in class	5			5			5			5		
	out of class	5			5			5					

Day Schools for the Deaf

Nursery and Infant Stage

9 Returns, including 1 with incomplete ticks*

		Children to Children			Children to Teachers			Teachers to Children			Child Care Staff		
		N	S	O	N	S	O	N	S	O	N	S	O
Natural Gesture	in class		2	7		2	6		3	5		4	4
	out of class		2	7		2	6		3	5			
Signs	in class	6	3		6	2		6	2		7	1	
	out of class	6	2	1	6	2		6	2				
Finger Spelling	in class	7	2		7	1		7	1		7	1	
	out of class	7	2		7	1		7	1				

Junior Stage

9 Returns, including 4 with incomplete ticks; of these 4, 1 had omissions under Child Care Staff Only*

		Children to Children			Children to Teachers			Teachers to Children			Child Care Staff		
		N	S	O	N	S	O	N	S	O	N	S	O
Natural Gesture	in class		5	4		4	4		5	3		4	4
	out of class		3	6		4	4		5	3			
Signs	in class	4	4	1	5	3		6	1		6	1	1
	out of class		8	1	3	5		7	1				
Finger Spelling	in class	4	5		4	4		5	3		6	1	
	out of class	4	3		5	1		5	1				

Secondary Stage

6 Returns, including 3 with incomplete ticks; of these 3, 1 had omissions under Child Care Staff Only*

		Children to Children			Children to Teachers			Teachers to Children			Child Care Staff		
		N	S	O	N	S	O	N	S	O	N	S	O
Natural Gesture	in class		4	2		4	1		2	3		1	3
	out of class		3	2		3	1		2	2			
Signs	in class	2	3	1	2	3		3	2		3	1	
	out of class		3	3	2	2	1	3	2				
Finger Spelling	in class		5	1	1	4		1	4		3	1	
	out of class	1	4	1	2	3		1	4				

* One School, in its return for each of the three stages, completed the column 'By Children to Children' only.

Day Schools for Deaf and Partially Hearing

Nursery and Infant Stage

10 Returns, including 4 with incomplete ticks; of these 4, 3 had omissions under Child Care Staff Only

		Children to Children			Children to Teachers			Teachers to Children			Child Care Staff		
		N	S	O	N	S	O	N	S	O	N	S	O
Natural Gesture	in class		5	5		8	2		9	1		5	2
	out of class		5	5		7	2		9				
Signs	in class	7	3			8	2		9	1		4	3
	out of class	7	3			8	2		9	1			
Finger Spelling	in class	10				9	1		9	1		6	1
	out of class	10				9	1		9	1			

Junior Stage

10 Returns, including 7 with incomplete ticks; of these 7, 5 had omissions under Child Care Staff only

		Children to Children			Children to Teachers			Teachers to Children			Child Care Staff		
		N	S	O	N	S	O	N	S	O	N	S	O
atural Gesture	in class		6	4		8	2	1(a)	8	1		3	2
	out of class		4	5		8	1	1(a)	7	1			
Signs	in class	4	5	1	5	5		10				4	1
	out of class	1	6	2	5	5		10					
Finger Spelling	in class	6	4		7	3		8	2			4	1
	out of class	5	5		7	3		8	2				

(a) One junior department (19 children) of an all age school

Secondary Stage

10 Returns, including 5 with incomplete ticks, under Child Care Staff Only

		Children to Children			Children to Teachers			Teachers to Children			Child Care Staff		
		N	S	O	N	S	O	N	S	O	N	S	O
Natural Gesture	in class		8	2	2	7	1	2	7	1		3	2
	out of class		5	5	2	7	1	2	8				
Signs	in class	2	6	2	6	3	1	10				4	1
	out of class		7	3	6	3	1	10					
Finger Spelling	in class	5	5		6	4		6	4			4	1
	out of class	4	6		5	5		5	5				

Boarding Schools for Deaf and Partially Hearing

Nursery and Infant Stage — 4 Returns

		Children to Children			Children to Teachers			Teachers to Children			Child Care Staff		
		N	S	O	N	S	O	N	S	O	N	S	O
Natural Gesture	in class		1	3		2	2		3	1	1	1	2
	out of class			4		1	3		3	1			
Signs	in class		4		1	3		4			2	2	
	out of class		4		1	3		4					
Finger Spelling	in class	4			4			4			3	1	
	out of class	4			4			4					

Junior Stage — 4 Returns

		Children to Children			Children to Teachers			Teachers to Children			Child Care Staff		
		N	S	O	N	S	O	N	S	O	N	S	O
Natural Gesture	in class		1	3		2	2		3	1		2	2
	out of class			4		2	2		3	1			
Signs	in class		3	1	4			2	2			4	
	out of class		1	3	4			2	2				
Finger Spelling	in class	4			4			1	3			4	
	out of class		3	1	4				4				

Secondary Stage — 4 Returns

		Children to Children			Children to Teachers			Teachers to Children			Child Care Staff		
		N	S	O	N	S	O	N	S	O	N	S	O
Natural Gesture	in class		3	1	4			4				3	1
	out of class			4	4			4					
Signs	in class		4		1	3		2	2			4	
	out of class		1	3		3	1	1	3				
Finger Spelling	in class		3	1	4			4				4	
	out of class		2	2	1	2	1	1	3				

Day Schools for Deaf and Partially Hearing

Nursery and Infant Stage 7 Returns

		Children to Children			Children to Teachers			Teachers to Children			Child Care Staff		
		N	S	O	N	S	O	N	S	O	N	S	O
Natural Gesture	in class		4	3		5	2	1(d)	5	1		6	1
	out of class		3	4		4	3	1(d)	5	1			
Signs	in class	4	3		5	2		7				6	1
	out of class	4	3		4	3		7					
Finger Spelling	in class	7			7			7			7		
	out of class	7			7			7					

Junior Stage 7 Returns

		Children to Children			Children to Teachers			Teachers to Children			Child Care Staff		
		N	S	O	N	S	O	N	S	O	N	S	O
Natural Gesture	in class		4	3		6	1	1(d)	6			6	1
	out of class		3	4		4	3	1(d)	6				
Signs	in class	4	3		5	2		7				6	1
	out of class	3	4		5	1	1	7					
Finger Spelling	in class	7			6	1		6	1			6	1
	out of class	7			7			7					

Secondary Stage 7 Returns

		Children to Children			Children to Teachers			Teachers to Children			Child Care Staff		
		N	S	O	N	S	O	N	S	O	N	S	O
Natural Gesture	in class		4	3		6	1	1(d)	6			6	1
	out of class		4	3		5	2	1(d)	6				
Signs	in class	4	3(a)	1(a)	6(b)	1	1(b)	7(c)		1(c)		6	1
	out of class	3	4(a)	1(a)	6(b)	1	1(b)	7(c)		1(c)			
Finger Spelling	in class	6	1		7(b)		1(b)	7(c)		1(c)		6	1
	out of class	6	1		7(b)		1(b)	7(c)		1(c)			

One school duplicated entries as indicated at (a) (b) and (c). They explained that 'Often' referred to one top class taught by a teacher who was at the school when finger spelling was officially used. The other entries refer to the other top class at the school.
The entries marked (d) all occur in the returns of one school.

SCOTLAND

Partially Hearing Units

Nursery and Infant Stage — **1 return**

		Children to Children			Children to Teachers			Teachers to Children			Child Care Staff		
		N	S	O	N	S	O	N	S	O	N	S	O
Natural Gesture	in class		1			1		1					
	out of class		1			1				1			1
Signs	in class		1				1		1				
	out of class		1				1		1			1	
Finger Spelling	in class	1			1			1					
	out of class	1			1			1			1		

Junior Stage — **2 returns**

		Children to Children			Children to Teachers			Teachers to Children			Child Care Staff		
		N	S	O	N	S	O	N	S	O	N	S	O
Natural Gesture	in class		1	1		2			2				
	out of class		1	1		2			2			1	1
Signs	in class	1	1		1	1		1	1				
	out of class	1	1		1	1		1	1		1	1	
Finger Spelling	in class	2			2			2					
	out of class	2			2			2			2		

Secondary Stage — **2 returns**

		Children to Children			Children to Teachers			Teachers to Children			Child Care Staff		
		N	S	O	N	S	O	N	S	O	N	S	O
Natural Gesture	in class		2			2			2				
	out of class		1	1		2			2			2	
Signs	in class	1	1		1	1		2					
	out of class	1	1		1	1		1	1		1	1	
Finger Spelling	in class	2			2			2					
	out of class	2			2			2			2		

An attempt to compare numbers of deaf school leavers with numbers of deaf adults known to welfare officers

(See Chapter XI, paragraph 219)

1. We attempted to establish a statistical basis for evidence suggesting that welfare officers to the deaf come into contact with the great majority of former pupils of schools for the deaf. Our intention was to compare the number of deaf adults on the register of handicapped persons (and therefore likely to be known to welfare officers and missioners) with the number of pupils who had left schools for the deaf over the relevant period.

Available Statistics

2. Annual Reports of the Ministry of Health include statistics of registration of deaf and hard-of-hearing persons, divided into the categories: (a) deaf without speech (b) deaf with speech (c) hard of hearing; and into the age groups: under age 16, 16–64, 65 and over. The three categories are defined as follows:

Deaf without Speech: Those who have no useful hearing and whose normal method of communication is by signs, finger spelling or writing.

Deaf with Speech: Those who (even with a hearing aid) have little or no useful hearing but whose normal method of communication is by speech and lipreading.

Hard-of-hearing: Those who (with or without a hearing aid) have some useful hearing and whose normal method of communication is by speech, listening and lipreading.

3. Annual Reports of the Department of Education and Science contain numbers of handicapped pupils classified by category of handicap and age last birthday. An approximate figure for the population passing through schools of the deaf could be obtained by taking the sum of 15 year old age groups over a period; the period chosen would have been that corresponding with the school years of the deaf adults on the register of handicapped persons. But detailed statistics of age-groups in special schools were not collected during the war years, or immediately after.

4. It would be possible to calculate the number of school leavers during the period 1947 to 1966 with the object of comparing this with the number of deaf adults in the relevant age groups (i.e. 16 to 36 years approximately) now on the register. But statistics are not available centrally showing numbers in each year of age on the register. The information could be obtained only through local authorities. For the following reasons we decided that the results of such an inquiry would contain too many uncertainties:

(a) Registration is according to the person's present condition and needs rather than according to the origin of his disability. The deaf with speech include a number of persons who became deaf after acquiring speech and language naturally, some of whom were educated in ordinary schools and did not lose their hearing until adult life.

(b) There appears to be reason to believe that there may be inconsistencies of classification. In the Report of the Ministry of Health for 1964 it was stated, 'The total number of deaf people registered varied little from the previous year, but within the total, there was a reduction of about 1,000 in the number classified as deaf with speech and a corresponding increase in the number classified as deaf without speech'.

The view of the Ministry of Health

5. The Ministry of Health, whom we consulted, were of the opinion that a valid statistical comparison would not be possible without an elaborate ad hoc enquiry. They also pointed out that although registration is likely to indicate that the person registered is well known to his

welfare worker it does not establish that this is the case, nor does it provide information about frequency of contact. However, from the experience of their professional advisers visiting welfare services throughout the country, they were of the opinion that in most areas of the country welfare officers and missioners do, in fact, come to know the great majority of former pupils from schools for the deaf. While in London there is a sufficiently great concentration of numbers of oral deaf adults to form a separate social organisation, this is still only a small proportion of the adult deaf, many of whom require some social help.

Figures represent paragraph numbers except where otherwise indicated.

Printed in England for Her Majesty's Stationery Office by Product Support (Graphics) Limited, Derby
Dd. 504483 K8 6/73